PRAISE FOR CLARITY:

This is the most well written, inspirational, no nonsense and smart book I have read in 30 years! If you want to rely on "chance" in life, don't read it. If you want to clearly and enthusiastically get from point A to Z, Steve has done a masterful job of capturing the road to success from his own experience getting there.

ERIC YAVERBAUM
Bestselling author of *Leadership Secrets of the World's Most Successful CEO's* and *PR for Dummies*

I knew from the age of six exactly what I wanted to do with my life, for those of you that don't have that clarity; this book will equip you to figure it out. I highly recommend you get it, read it and apply it to your life.

BRETT BUTLER
Former Major League Baseball Player and Coach, and author of *Field of Hope*

Engaging, entertaining, and incredibly insightful are all words that I would use to describe both Steven Cesari and his excellent book.

MICHAEL T. MURRAY, N.D.
Author of the *Encyclopedia of Natural Medicine* and 30 other books

There are so many useful and powerful concepts in this book and those that resonate most with me are "Finding Balance" and "Understanding the Why." Steve has created a roadmap for success in life and made it easy to navigate. You will thank yourself for reading *Clarity*. Enjoy the journey!

PETER ROBY
Athletic Director, Northeastern University

As an entrepreneur, I have learned the critical importance of establishing priorities and maintaining a clear and consistent focus to reach profitability and success. This book presents workable strategies for readers who want to gain a clearer understanding of who they are and how they can work toward their greatest purpose.

DEEDEE MORRISON

Founder, CEO, Private Air/Private Shoppes

A balanced life is not the same for any two individuals. We are all wired differently but being clear on what "balance" is for YOUR life is critical to achieve the levels of success you seek. Steve has laid out a great framework in this book that will assist you in finding your balance, purpose and the confidence to pursue what is right for YOU.

READ DAVIS

President, McGriff, Seibels & Williams, Inc.

I have known Steve for more than 7 years and in that time I have seen him personally transform the lives of countless men and couples in our community. Steve has a knack for getting to the heart of the matter and helping people get clear on what they need to do to change their lives. This book is engaging, challenging and practical. If you are ready for change, I recommend you pick up this book and start reading.

VIC PENTZ

Senior Pastor, Peachtree Presbyterian Church

It is quite amazing how much time we spend developing strategic plans in business...and how little time we spend understanding and implementing God's plans and purpose for our personal lives! Steve is one of the most passionate and energetic leaders I know, and you won't want to miss out on his story and life lessons about how we can live that way too!

BONNIE WURZBACHER

Senior Vice President, The Coca-Cola Company

I became a billionaire by surrounding myself with the right people and taking actions on my dreams. Nothing happens in life until you take action. This book gives you a clear concise roadmap to take your life, business and your relationship to the next level. I highly recommend that you TAKE ACTION and buy Steve's book.

BILL BARTMANN

NY Times bestselling author of *Bailout Riches* and National Entrepreneur of the year

When I was a rookie with the Dallas Cowboys in 1965, I was exposed to goals by Tom Landry. He believed strongly that you had to have goals set each and every day to be a champion. In this book Steve has really done a great job of helping you learn how to set goals for your life personally and professionally. He helps you focus so clearly in all areas of your life, mentally, physically and spiritually. Goals have been a big part of my life. I wish I had the knowledge in this book when I was a young man.

DAN REEVES

Legendary NFL player and coach

CLARITY

Dave,

Your Success blesses others.

Iron Sharpens Iron

CLARITY

How to get it

How to keep it &

How to use it to

BALANCE YOUR LIFE

STEVEN CESARI

Published by Advantage, Charleston, South Carolina.
Member of Advantage Media Group.

ADVANTAGE is a registered trademark and the Advantage colophon is a trademark of Advantage Media Group, Inc.

Printed in the United States of America.

ISBN: 978-1-59932-214-8
LCCN: 2010915922

This publication is designed to provide accurate and authoritative information in regard to the subject matter covered. It is sold with the understanding that the publisher is not engaged in rendering legal, accounting, or other professional services. If legal advice or other expert assistance is required, the services of a competent professional person should be sought.

Advantage Media Group is proud to be a part of the Tree Neutral™ program. Tree Neutral offsets the number of trees consumed in the production and printing of this book by taking proactive steps such as planting trees in direct proportion to the number of trees used to print books. To learn more about Tree Neutral, please visit www.treeneutral.com. To learn more about Advantage's commitment to being a responsible steward of the environment, please visit www.advantagefamily.com/green

Advantage Media Group is a leading publisher of business, motivation, and self-help authors. Do you have a manuscript or book idea that you would like to have considered for publication? Please visit www.amgbook.com or call 1.866.775.1696

To my family,

my wife Indy—
"You are still my one in a million"

and my children: Courtney, Stefany, Whitney, and Matthew—
I am proud to be your dad.

ACKNOWLEDGEMENTS

So many people work behind the scenes to bring a book to life that it's virtually impossible to name them all, but I want to recognize a few who made this book a reality. Thank you to all the creative people at Advantage Media: Adam Witty, Michelle Pyle, Brooke White, and George Stevens. Thanks also to my editors, Denis Boyles and Ron Geraci. Denis captured the vision and Ron created the outline, then listened to my stories, sharpened my words and kept me focused.

To Chuck and my band of brothers at IRONMEN and to our couples groups, you were all a constant source of encouragement and accountability. Iron truly does sharpen iron. A special thanks to Laura Poe, who kept me motivated and on task.

Thank you to my former business partner, Tommy Newberry, who directly and indirectly developed some of the concepts in this book.

A heartfelt thank you to my mom and dad, and my brothers and sisters—Albert, Lucille, Linda, Jimmy, Cheryl, Susan, Rick, David, and John. You have all helped to mold me into the man I am today. I love you all and miss you very much. To my in-laws, George and Eleanor Soos, whose determination and integrity I try to model every day.

To my beautiful wife, Indy, who is my biggest fan and source of encouragement. She listened to my stories, proofread manuscripts, supported me through the process and kept me focused on the goal. She made this a better book and she has made me a better man. I am eternally grateful and I will love you always.

To my children—Courtney, Stefany, Whitney and Matthew, whose lives exemplify the principles in this book. I love you guys and you are all an inspiration to me.

Most of all, I want to thank God for giving me the wisdom and experiences I shared in this book and the courage to take action on my dream, to make a positive impact—at home, at work and in the world.

TABLE OF CONTENTS

INTRODUCTION

If you don't know where you're going,
any road—or ocean—will take you there.

When I was in college, during the mid 1970s, I got a call from my brother-in-law in New York, Bob Pontz. He said, "I'm taking my sailboat down to Bimini," which is one of the small islands in the Bahamas about 90 miles off the coast of Florida.

He asked if I wanted to come along as part of the crew on a 32-foot-long sloop called *Narcissus*.

I was 21 years old. And it took me half a second to answer him.

"Are you kidding me?" I said. "I would love to!"

When you think about being on a sailboat and sailing to the Bahamas, what picture comes to mind?

All I could envision was lying on the bow of the boat, basking in the sun, drinking beer, pulling into port, and—this was before I was married—finding a bar or a party and having the time of my life.

The only problem? My brother-in-law planned this trip in September, which is the start of the storm season. I later found out that this meant sudden wind shifts, small craft warnings and six-to-eight-foot waves much of the time.

There were, including me, four people on the boat: Captain Bob, his 22-year-old brother Corky, and Jeff, who was one of Captain Bob's buddies.

The trip started out beautifully. I'll never forget when we set sail from Mamaroneck, New York. I was standing on the bow of the sailboat on that narrow plank of wood with the chrome railing going around it. Everything seemed perfect. I was ready to start an amazing trip.

Then the fog rolled in.

I couldn't see a foot in front of me. And that wasn't a great situation, because my job was to look out for any junk floating in the water, to make sure we didn't run into it.

As we sailed out past the Throgs Neck Bridge, I remember the rain coming down so hard it was actually knocking the weatherproofing right off my rain jacket. Within five minutes, I was soaked. I was beginning to regret that I had come on this sailing trip—but I tried hard to keep an optimistic attitude, figuring we would get through this unexpected rough patch and be laughing about it in no time. I was on the boat, and there was no going back, so I was still hoping for a magnificent experience.

Conditions improved as we sailed our way eastward. We finally made it out to the Atlantic Ocean and were greeted by a couple of days of perfect weather. I thought the rough start to the journey was now behind us, and it would be smooth sailing from then on. It was absolutely gorgeous as we sailed in the evening with the moon shining on the ocean, and the plankton lighting up like fireworks as our bow cut through the water.

Everything was beautiful. Life was good.

As for crew duties, we all took four-hour shifts manning the helm. When you're sitting at the helm of the boat, you're responsible for keeping it on course. Even if you've never been on a large sailboat for several days, I'm sure you can imagine a problem that sailors have been dealing with for thousands of years: You tend to get sleepy. When you are staring at the compass and it's 2 a.m., the rocking motion of the boat makes you doze off. The other man on watch is supposed to keep you awake, but he's usually dozing off, too. So you wake with a jolt to see your incorrect compass reading and wonder how long you've been going in the wrong direction.

This happened to me several times. I would try to get back on course without making a fuss, because I didn't want the other guys to know I had fallen asleep. And this was usually no big deal because, up to this point, we were always within sight of land and could see the lights on shore. After a few shifts at the helm, out on those gorgeous nights, I felt I was actually getting the hang of it.

After sailing for several days, we pulled into port in Morehead City, North Carolina, to replenish our supplies. As we left Morehead City—remember this name, please—and headed back out to sea, we had to go past an area known as Frying Pan Shoals.

The Frying Pan Shoals are a large area of sandbars and gravel bars about 50 miles off of the North Carolina coast. These shoals have been a hazard to ships since the beginning of European exploration and they're still treacherous today. The area is littered with wrecks. In fact, from May 1994 to August 2008, over 130 new shipwreck locations were discovered there.

Of course, I didn't know any of this at the time. I learned it after the trip.

To steer clear of this peril, we set a course 50 nautical miles east from Morehead City. This meant that, for the first time on the trip, we would *not be in sight of land.*

As I mentioned, I only learned how dangerous Frying Pan Shoals were *after* the trip. They meant nothing whatsoever to me at the time we were sailing past them. There was one other piece of extremely interesting information not then known to me: This was Captain Bob's maiden voyage as the captain of a boat in the open sea.

His maiden voyage!

If I had known this before I went on the trip, do you think I would have gone?

Even though I was in my twenties at the time, and was no stranger to taking stupid risks, I'm pretty sure I would have said, "uh... no thanks."

When inexperience meets a hazardous situation, things can turn bad quickly.

And indeed they did. Right around midnight.

I was below in my berth, fast asleep and dreaming about partying in the Bahamas. Suddenly, I was thrown off my bed and hit the ceiling—which was the underside of the deck in the bow of the boat. We had gone over a huge wave. Half-awake and somewhat shocked, I started climbing the steps to get up on the deck, and heard Captain Bob yell out, "Measurements!" Another voice yelled back: "25 fathoms! 10 fathoms! 30 feet! 15 feet! 8 feet!"

We were out in the middle of the ocean, 50 nautical miles from land. And we were in 8 feet of water.

As I came up on deck, there was white water everywhere. Waves were rolling around the boat, tossing us like a cork. I thought we were going to die. As I became fully aware of what was happening, and realized this was not a dream, fear swept through my body. I had never been so frightened in my life.

I heard Captain Bob yelling something to the effect of, "Prepare to come about!"

I said, "Come about?! Are you crazy?! Get us outta here!"

He made some maneuver and we managed to get clear of the white water. Finally, the sea calmed. But in the all the turbulence and confusion, a small piece of electronics called a radio directional finder, or RDF, was knocked off a shelf and broken. In the mid 1970s, well before the modern days of GPS, an RDF used radio waves to determine a vessel's location at sea. It locates two radio frequencies on shore and then triangulates them with the boat to calculate where you are.

With the RDF broken, we had no idea where we were. Does *Gilligan's Island* ring a bell?

So now we had to figure out a plan of action. We agreed that from this point forward we would "captain by committee." We decided by consensus that the best course was to head due west until we hit land.

I thought we were doomed. Unfortunately, I had just read a book about the Bermuda Triangle and here we were, right in the middle of it. In the weeks before the trip I had also watched the movie *Jaws*. I kept replaying one of the famous lines over and over in my head: "So, 1,100 men went in the water, 316 men came out and the sharks took the rest."

We were towing a two-man life raft behind our sailboat because there was no room for it on deck. All I could picture was our sailboat going down, and me without a seat in the little raft because I was the biggest guy. I had visions of hanging onto this raft as sharks started to feast on me. All I could think was: "How did I get myself into this mess? I'm just a college kid looking for a good time in the Bahamas!"

I was really, really, really afraid.

And things would get much worse.

When you're in the open sea and have no clue where you are, Murphy's Law starts to apply in sadistic ways. As we headed west in search of land, the weather started to worsen again. The skies clouded, rain fell and the wind began to blow. The sea became turbulent. The waves were colossal. I was told they were 12- to-14-footers. As we came up and over each wave, there was a wall of water in front of us and a wall of water behind us.

After a full day heading due west in this weather, we still did not see land or any other boats or ships. At this point, Captain Bob told me to get on the radio and send out a distress signal.

"This is sloop *Narcissus!* Mayday! Mayday! Mayday!"

I said this for hours on end into a microphone, to no avail. Even when the bad weather finally subsided, I kept on with the distress signals.

Then there was the little issue of food and water. Remember, we only had two days worth of supplies on board, because we were planning on coming into port to restock every two days. We made the decision to ration the food and the drinks we had, and this added to the already tense situation.

For two full days we sailed westward, without any sign of land or other ships. We were literally lost at sea and running low on food and water. Day three came and went, and still no land sightings. I began to wonder if we would ever see land again. I thought about my life and started to negotiate with God. I didn't have a very strong faith back then, but the saying is true: "There are no atheists in foxholes." I started praying, asking God to get us through this mess.

By day four, we were down to the end of our rations. We had some fruit and a six-pack of Diet Doctor Pepper. We called it "DDP" and to this day, I cannot bring myself to drink it again.

At about noon on day four, we saw a bird. Not a seagull but a regular bird. We all got very excited; *land must be near*! Later that day, at about 4:00 p.m., the weather worsened again. But this time it was a blessing. When lightning lit up the horizon, we could see the distant outline of the shore. Finally, after four and a half days of fear and misery at sea, and completely out of food and water, we found land. We sailed into port, thanking God to be alive. We all jumped off the sailboat and got down and kissed the ground.

We were in Morehead City, right where we had started several days before.

LACK OF CLARITY IS THE ROOT OF MOST FAILURES

Let me make this clear: This story is a reflection of my life, and quite possibly yours.

We all set off on our big adventure, without paying much attention to where we're going, how we're going to get there, or if we have the people and resources we're going to need to make it happen. As a result, we end up drifting through life and reacting to our circumstances as they happen, rather than clearly defining where we want to go and surrounding ourselves with the right people and resources to achieve our dreams.

Wandering through life without a clear destination or a plan to get there is just like drifting in a sailboat and letting the winds and currents carry you wherever they may be going.

All of this is due to lack of clarity. More specifically, not having a clearly defined vision of where you want to go.

I know this very well. I spent most of my life drifting like the sloop *Narcissus* out in the Atlantic. I made wrong turns and bad decisions because I lacked a clear vision of what I really wanted to accomplish and who I wanted to become.

Once I transitioned from wandering aimlessly and really started to practice the principles in this book, life got on course. I surrounded myself with the right people and I got extreme clarity about my purpose and passion in life. The creation of a $100 million business was just one manifestation of having this clarity. Others were more personal. When I achieved extreme clarity and passion about what it meant to be a dad and what it meant to be a husband, it set me on the path to celebrate 30 years of marriage with my wife Indy—and to be a father of four grown children who are achieving their own purpose and passion in life.

In short, I had been drifting—and I'll tell you much more about those years in the chapters ahead—until I learned to live my life differently—with clarity, purpose and intentionality. I've learned to help other people live their lives that same way. Along the way I've developed a knack for helping people and companies identify their key issues, so that they can move toward clarity, unlock their potential, and create the results they want. I've done this with Fortune 500 companies and with entrepreneurs. I've done this with NFL and college football teams. I've done this with couples and high school students. And I can do it with you.

That's why I've written this book.

When you implement the principles I explain in this book, they will help to bring clarity and balance to your personal and business life. You will experience a transformation that will boost your confidence and take you places you never imagined you could go.

IT'S LIKE MAPQUEST FOR LIFE

You know the MapQuest website, don't you? The other day I was looking for directions and, not knowing how to get to my destination, I typed two addresses into MapQuest.

All I had to do was type in the location I was starting from, and then enter the destination I wanted to reach, and click a button. In a few seconds, I printed out a step-by-step map to take me there. Everything was laid out for me in a clear, concise manner.

Wouldn't it be great if there was MapQuest for life? Imagine if you could tell a website or some other service where you want to go, or what you want to do, and then, in a few seconds—bingo!—it would provide a detailed, step-by-step map to take you there.

To my knowledge, no such website exists. Likewise, there is no easy, quick way to gain clarity about your passion and purpose in life. But the principles I've laid out in this book are as close as you can get to having a MapQuest for life. They represent a proven system that can keep you on a steady course and save you significant time, energy and money.

When you apply this system to your business, your marriage, your family, your relationships, your health...to *any* aspect of your life, it will provide a clear map to take you from where you currently are to where you want to go. You'll have to apply the dedication and the effort to take the journey. But you'll have a map in hand.

Here's the first empowering secret to keep in mind as you begin this journey: When you get clear about the person you want to become and what you want to accomplish, *you will attract the things you need to make it happen.*

How do I know? I married one of those precious things. On my second date with Indy, I asked her what she wanted to do in life. Without hesitating, she said, "I want to have four children before I'm 30, I want to get my Master's Degree in Speech and Language Pathology in five years and my doctorate in ten years."

Then she asked what I wanted to do.

I said, "I think want to marry you!"

Indy was crystal clear. She had extreme clarity in her vision of what she wanted to accomplish with her life. She knew what her purpose was and she was passionate about doing it. Today, we have four children, and she has a doctorate in Speech and Language Pathology.

I'll say it again: When you have clarity in your life, and you know what your purpose is and what you want to accomplish, it's amazing how you'll attract the right people and resources you need to make that happen.

Most people lack this clarity.

We see it in marriages. Consider that about 40 percent of all marriages end in divorce. Most couples spend more time planning their wedding than they do planning their marriages! They have a clear picture of what they want out of their wedding, and what they want their wedding to look like—but they don't have a clue what they want their marriage to look like.

We see it in our jobs. When two million people were surveyed, *84 percent* said they hated doing what they did for a living. They didn't have clarity when they were seeking a profession, and now they have no sense of purpose or passion for what they are doing.

We see it in our financial lives. Look at the scourge of credit card debt and overspending that is affecting so many people in this country. Did you know more than 70 percent of the U.S. population will retire without enough money to support themselves and will be dependent on somebody else?

We see it in our health. We have an absolute health epidemic going on right now: More than one million Americans will die this year from heart attack, stroke and cancer caused by poor lifestyle choices. Public health experts say that 80 percent of them could be saved by eating right and exercising, and by having a clear vision of a healthier lifestyle.

FAILURE IS A RESULT OF NOT HAVING A CLEAR AND CONCISE PLAN

Remember, nobody plans to fail. Failure is a result of not having a clear and concise plan. And our failure to plan is not always due to laziness or lack of forethought. Nowadays, it's easy to be overloaded. There's too much to do and not enough time to do it. Modern technology has exposed us to more daily information than previous generations could have imagined. But how do we discern what to listen to and what to tune out—and whom to listen to and whom to tune out? **The modern world makes the focused life seem almost impossible.** Life is like a smorgasbord with endless choices, and we keep going back and stuffing ourselves with everything that's there *because we do not have clarity.*

Clarity is the remedy. It's found in setting wise goals and tuning out other distractions. Clarity will tell your brain what to focus on and what to tune out. Clarity will tell you whom to focus on and whom to tune out. Clarity will minimize the distractions. Clarity will act as your GPS to take you where you want to go. That's why the main mission of this book is to show you how to achieve clarity and bring balance to your life.

WHAT ARE THE TWO MOST IMPORTANT DAYS OF YOUR LIFE?

I had the pleasure of meeting General Russel L. Honoré. He's a three-star general who was in charge of the initial response to Hurricane Katrina in New Orleans. On the day I met him, he was recalling an episode in which one of his mentors asked, "What are the two most important days in life?" The response his mentor gave is one that should resonate with all of us.

"Number one is the day you were born."

"Number two is the day you figure out *why* you were born."

My sincere hope and desire is that after reading this book, you will be closer to understanding why you were born and have greater clarity toward understanding your purpose and passion in life.

CHAPTER 1

WE ARE ALL TERMINAL—DON'T ACCELERATE THE PROCESS

"If I knew I was going to live this long, I'd have taken better care of myself."

MICKEY MANTLE

I want to share a secret with you. If you violate one extremely important principle in life, you are guaranteed to fail—no matter what type of business you're in, what type of product or service you provide, or how well capitalized you are.

If you violate this principle, you are guaranteed to fail in both business and life.

This principle is very simple: **Don't die.**

Now, don't take this the wrong way. I know people die every day, and it's an inevitable part of life. But a lot of people needlessly *accelerate the process* of making their own death occur. And they die far too soon and much too young. That's the principle I'm talking about here.

My dad violated this principle when he was 46 years old.

My dad was a hard-working guy. He worked about 70 hours a week at his job as the owner of a grocery store in Valhalla, New York. He didn't take care of his health, and he smoked two packs of Camel (unfiltered) cigarettes every day. He was responsible for sustaining a family of eight children, and I can't imagine the pressure he must have felt financially, and in many other ways, in dealing with those responsibilities. Perhaps he smoked because he thought it would help him deal with the stress he was facing as a father and a provider.

My dad's death left a huge void in my life, and in the lives of my brothers and sisters and my mom. Let me tell you about the day he passed away.

It was July of 1968. I was 13 years old, on summer break before starting the ninth grade. It was a Sunday morning, and we were getting ready to go to church. My dad started feeling a little dizzy. It was a very hot, humid day so my mom told him to sit in the room that was air-conditioned. But his dizziness became progressively worse.

My mom called our pharmacist, Mr. Slotnik. He was a good family friend and owned the business right next to my dad's grocery store. He said he'd come right over. My dad's symptoms still worsened, so my mom called our family doctor, Dr. Ryan. This was back in the days when doctors made house calls, so he said he'd come right over, too. As we were waiting for Mr. Slotnik and Dr. Ryan to arrive, my dad's eyes rolled to the back of his head and he lost consciousness. We carried him to the back of our station wagon to take him to the hospital.

He was laying in my lap in the back of the car. I was a Boy Scout and had learned to do CPR and mouth-to-mouth resuscitation, and I was trying to perform both on my dad. But he didn't regain consciousness. When we arrived at the hospital, we rushed him in and the nurses and the doctors came out. It was like a scene on TV: They brought him into that little room, they closed the curtains and they hooked him up to a machine that beeped in time with his heart rate. I'll never forget that. It's emblazoned in my memory.

The beeps from the machine became slower.

Beep-beep-beep-beep. Beeep. Beeeeep. Beeeeeeep.

Then they stopped.

The doctors and nurses came out from behind the curtains. One of them said, "Your dad didn't make it." I was confused, in shock, and wondering how this was possible. My father had seemed perfectly healthy two hours before and now he was gone.

While I remember every detail up to this moment, the hours and days that follow are largely blank. I remember going back home and friends and family coming around to console us. But I was in a daze, simply trying to make sense of what had just happened to our family. And what had just happened to me.

THE LETTER

About 20 years after my dad's death, I received a copy of a letter that my mom had received during that summer in 1968. This letter was written by a friend and business associate of my dad's. I learned more about my father from this letter than from all the other people and stories combined. And although I didn't fully realize it when I first read it, over time I came to view this letter as part of a road map that would help guide me through life. I would like to share this letter with you, along with some of the lessons and wisdom it has given me.

Dear Linda, Jimmy, Cheryl, Susan, Steve, Ricky, John and David,

As you know by now, your father has many, many friends. He has been taken from all these friends but especially from each of you. There's no replacement for this loss. Now you have only the courage God can give. I would hope each of you will be able, over time, to face the fact of your loss without bitterness, be able to accept life, be able to cherish all the fine memories your dad leaves with all of us.

Each of you needs to do his part to behave in a manner that would bring pride to your father if he were still with us and to bring pride to your mother whose loss is at least as great as yours, and who needs your help at every turn. Most of all, you should know that to those outside your family, your father was more than a friend, more than a businessman, more than a member of a local organization. He was a very special person. He was ahead of his years in anticipating the needs of his community and taking action to meet those needs. He was a counselor and a friend to those who came to him with trouble.

He had personal magic, the kind that gave a lift to those he met each day and made him a person who was refreshing to be with. As you get older you will become aware that his life, in the sight of both God and man, was one of fine accomplishment that his contributions were greater than those who were granted many extra years, that the community in which you live is a much better one because of him. I loved him, too.

Archie Bowes, Jr.

Reading this letter always makes me emotional. On this very day, even more so. I'm actually writing these words on Father's Day.

It's an understatement to say that I'm extremely happy that I have this letter. Most people aren't lucky enough to have such an eloquent tribute to their lost parent. Of course, I would much rather have learned these details about my dad first-hand. But he left too soon for that.

THEN AND NOW

For my dad, on that summer day in 1968, my attempts at CPR were too little, too late. The damage had been done. He made choices that damaged his health—though he had access to much less information about how to maintain proper health, fitness and nutrition than we do today.

And that's a difference I can't ignore.

Given this, it's certainly no accident that I gravitate toward businesses that deal with health and fitness. My brother Rick and I started Trillium Health Products in 1989, marketing a product called the *Juiceman Juicer*—which sold millions of units. I wanted to devote my energies to a business that helped people make positive decisions about their health, and helped them extend their lives through those positive decisions so they might avoid my father's fate. As a child, I couldn't help my dad, but as an adult, I am passionate about helping others live healthy and successful lives.

That's why I've put this chapter first.

If you don't follow the principles in this chapter, *nothing else matters*. Sure, you can have a great impact on this planet even if your life is short; I believe my father did. Certainly, you can have poor health, or even be confined to a wheelchair or a bed, and still touch many people's lives. But I firmly believe that you must do everything you can *reasonably do* to improve and safeguard your health, your strength, and your energy in order to be effective in life. And today, you can do a great deal. We now have an incredible amount of information about how to live a high-energy, healthy lifestyle. And I'm going to give you the basic tools to do that.

It's important to understand that this isn't just about you. Our poor choices have consequences for those who depend on us.

In our day-to-day lives, it's very difficult to have a positive impact on others if you don't have the energy and vitality to use your talents. Further, there is a direct correlation between making good, healthy lifestyle choices and making good choices in other areas of life. More than any other factor, an unhealthy lifestyle will cause you to perform poorly in many key areas of life. After all, if you are run down, tired and out-of-balance, your ability to make good choices is compromised.

I see this every day. I recently met yet another person who is struggling in business and has poor health—and thinks his business trouble is causing his health issues. In his case, I believe, it's the other way around. Quite frequently, when a person like this man starts making better choices about his or her health, it has a ripple effect. They have more energy and vigor, and essential tasks that languished begin to get done. Fewer mistakes are made. Others place more confidence in them. It's a cycle of improvement, and one that's quite gratifying to watch. At this point, however, this man hasn't begun that turnaround. And I know what he's dealing with, because I've been there.

Some of the worst decisions I have ever made, in business and in life, were made when I was extremely run down. And they hurt me for long periods of time. The opposite is also true; some of my best decisions have come when I was in great shape both physically and emotionally.

If you will follow the steps I have outlined in this chapter, you can and will achieve a healthy, high-energy lifestyle. There is only one catch: I can't do it for you. You have to implement it and make it happen.

SIX STRATEGIES FOR HEALTHY, HIGH-ENERGY LIFESTYLE

If you get nothing else from this book, I hope you'll put these six strategies into action. Why? Because if you follow all of the other principles I talk about in the book but ignore these six strategies, you're almost guaranteed to fail. You'll be engineering your life to violate the same important principle that my dad did. Doing so can negate all of your positive efforts in all other areas of your life, no matter how hard you work.

1. Create a clear vision for the healthy lifestyle you want.

Again, it all comes down to clarity. Answer these two questions:

A. When you say you want to "have a healthy lifestyle," what specific goals and achievements does that entail? What does it really look like? Make it simple and specific, and write those goals down.

B. How long do you really want to live? (Have you ever even thought about this?)

My own written goal is stated like this: "I weigh 205 pounds and my body fat is 20 percent or less." Use whatever works for you. For me, having a picture of what I am aspiring to do helps me stay focused and helps me maintain a clear, concise picture of what I'm trying to accomplish. Notice that the goal is written in the present tense and stated with certainty, as if it was already accomplished; I'll explain why in an upcoming chapter.

Visual aids help. I have a picture of myself from 1986, when I ran the 10K Peachtree Road Race in Atlanta, Georgia in under 40 minutes. I was in the best shape of my life, or very close to it, and I continue to use that photo as a visual reminder of why I want to stay in shape.

As for the second question, take it seriously. If you want to live to be 90 years old, what habits will help you achieve this, and what habits will hold you back? The best way to look at this is to take a sheet of paper and draw a line down the middle. On the left side, write down everything that is negatively holding you back. On the right side, write down all the positive habits that will help you get there. Once you've done this, you can start to work on getting rid of the negative habits and replacing them with the positive ones.

Can you reach extreme old age without planning? Certainly. It happens all the time, as a walk through any nursing home will reveal. I'd like to live to be 101, myself, but I'd rather not join the ranks of people who didn't arrive at that age ready to tackle its adversities.

2. Create and sustain a positive mental attitude.

It is not what happens to us in life; it is how we respond to what is happening to us that really counts. Having a healthy, high-energy lifestyle requires that you create and sustain a positive mental attitude. It is not enough to have a clear goal if you are already telling yourself that you can't do it. I call that *stinkin' thinkin'*.

An irony? All stressful or negative emotions begin as a stressful or negative thought. The inability to deal with stress and worry has been linked to a multitude of illnesses, including depression, heart attack, cancer, ulcers and chronic fatigue, to name just a few.

Studies show that over 75 percent of illness can be linked to what I term *stinkin' thinkin'*. In other words, we cause over three quarters of our illnesses in our mind. Remember, stress and worry only exist to the degree that you allow them to exist. They are products of perception; it is the *way you think about something* that actually makes it stressful.

> "Your attitude, not your aptitude, will help determine your altitude in life."
>
> ZIG ZIGLAR

Here's an example. My father-in-law, George Soos, had triple bypass surgery last year at age 77. George was in very poor health. He was about 60 pounds overweight. He drank a few cocktails every day to help alleviate his chronic arthritic pain. George's doctor gave him a workout plan prior to his operation to help him get in shape for the operation, but he saw little point in following it. He had a very wary attitude going into the surgery.

Understand that George had spent much of his life being the epitome of good health and productive living. He was a starting defensive lineman for West Point back in 1954, and then a successful and honest politician who ran on the same ticket as Nelson Rockefeller. He was an executive with Long Island Lighting and later served as the County Clerk for the town of Roslyn, New York. He had vigorous health, but he began to lose it as he pursued his career and stopped taking care of himself. Diet was a large issue; *the older we get, the harder it becomes to overcome poor dietary habits with exercise.*

A few weeks after the surgery, my wife and I flew to New York to see him. When I asked him how he was doing, he said, "Steven, I never should have let them operate. I should have let God take me." I was shocked to hear this.

My wife and I and other family members continued to support and encourage him and give him a multitude of reasons why we and others still needed him around. Slowly but surely, George fought through the *stinkin' thinkin'* that had all but destroyed his will to live. He slowly regained the can-do attitude that served him so well in his life. He had to look inside himself and *take action*.

To recuperate, he started with just five minutes of exercise on a recumbent bike each day. He slowly worked up to 10 minutes, and then 15, and then 20 minutes each day. At the same time, he stopped drinking and started to eat healthier. He began keeping a journal of his food intake, exercise and weight loss; and he still keeps the journal. As of the writing of this book, at 78 years old, George has lost over 60 pounds and is—for the first time since his West Point playing days— less than 200 pounds!

George demonstrated quite vividly to me that our attitudes can either make us or break us. If you will take time to reflect on your situation and choose to respond with a positive mental attitude—rather than react with *stinkin' thinkin'*—you will be able to handle anything life throws your way.

3. Remember this formula: 75 + 20 + 5 = a healthy lifestyle.

What is it? Well, I've heard almost every concept in existence to create a healthy lifestyle, and this is the one that ultimately worked for me.

Here's what it means: **75 percent of our health comes from nutrition, 20 percent comes from exercise and five percent comes from supplements.**

The problem? Most people want to reverse this formula. They want to eat poorly, never exercise, and then—when they really need to—take a pill that will give them health (as well as a fit and trim body). Fortunes have been made on selling this erroneous premise. Years ago, there was actually a product called "Exercise in a Bottle," and the marketing suggested that taking this pill would deliver all the benefits of exercise. People didn't fall for something so obviously ridiculous, right? I'll answer that by telling you the product grew into a $100 million company.

THE SEVEN KEYS TO EATING WELL

Just how important is it to eat well? According to the "75 + 20 + 5 = a healthy lifestyle," nutrition is the most influential factor to your health, *by far*. It is the single most important factor in determining how much vitality and vigor we have in our lives—and how long we'll ultimately enjoy our stay on earth. Again, think of nutrition as anything that passes between your lips. The food we eat is the fuel for our bodies.

To illustrate this, I'd like to share the story of a friend who was in a hurry to get to his son's soccer game. He stopped at a gas station and filled his car with gas. He got to the game, but when he was driving home his car broke down. As it turned out, he was in such a rush that he put diesel fuel in his new Audi and caused $6,000 worth of damage. He had to replace the catalytic converter and many other parts.

Our bodies react the same way to the fuel we put in it. We are usually in such a rush; we put the wrong fuel in our body. Although it may not happen suddenly, the body will break down as a result. And $6,000 won't come close to fixing it. I can promise you that.

The consequences of poor nutrition are rampant today. Obesity and juvenile diabetes are at epidemic levels. Health experts are now emphasizing a terrifying possibility: **For the first time in U.S. history, the current generation of children might not outlive their parents.**

There are several reasons for this. For one, eating has become something that we do to entertain ourselves rather than to provide healthy fuel for our bodies. This sad fact has opened a ready path for many companies to sell products that exploit our bad habits, and has allowed misinformation to spread. Take dieting; people spend billions of dollars on commercial diets each year. The irony? Statistics show that almost 100 percent of the people regain 110 percent of whatever weight they lost within 12 months of going off the diet.

The message in that particular case is very simple: Diets don't work. So, what does work? It's pretty simple. Making the right choices about what we eat, so that our daily nutrition *supports* (rather than sabotages) our goal of having a healthy, energetic lifestyle.

Okay, back to the "75 + 20 + 5 = a healthy lifestyle" formula. It means that **75 percent** of our health and vitality comes from what passes between our lips. If we're not intentional and focused about what we eat, it's all too easy to give our bodies a mix of fuel that harms us. With proper nutrition, you can prevent a lot of the major degenerative diseases that occur commonly in the U.S. In fact, research has shown that over 80 percent of the deaths from the three top killers—heart attack, stroke and cancer—could be prevented with dietary changes.

Proper nutrition is so important to our lives, I'd like to share a mini-plan with you to make certain you have the tools you need to get a handle on the this often-misunderstood essential concept. Here are seven keys to eating well:

1. Have a plan. Again, it all starts with clarity. Being clear on what you need to accomplish with your diet, and having a daily plan to achieve those results, is the foundation of living a healthy, high-energy nutritional lifestyle. When you take the time to plan your meals, you are more likely to make wise choices that produce health and well-being.

Of course, most of us have such hectic, busy lifestyles that we usually wing it when it comes to our meals. At the very least, have a plan when you *buy* your food. It is a proven fact that when you go into the grocery store and you have a well-thought-out list, you will spend less time and money than if you went in unprepared. It is so important to be proactive and have clarity when it comes to preparing your meals.

2. Eat less animal meat and animal byproducts. The major source of cholesterol and fat in the American diet comes from animal and animal byproducts. This includes meat, cheese, ice cream...yes, all the things we love. There are a multitude of healthier alternatives today to these foods, and if you can just think about replacing some of them, you'll be taking a very positive step. For example, you can replace red meats with fish or poultry alternatives, which can be leaner sources of protein and will be more energizing to our body with less negative impact.

3. Consume five to nine servings of fruits and vegetables each day. If you don't even come close to this, you're very similar to most Americans who are slowly allowing their bodies to weaken and develop degenerative diseases. The reality is that less than 10 percent of the population gets the recommended servings of fruits and vegetables each day. This disturbing fact is what created the opportunity for my brother and me to start Trillium Health Products, marketers of the *Juiceman Juicer.*

Do I really "juice?" You bet I do. My family started juicing 20 years ago and we still do it every day. Before working on this chapter today, I got up early and I had my usual glass of pineapple/orange/grapefruit/strawberry juice. I don't feel that I can get the right start to a good day unless I have all of those nutrients from the fruits and vegetables in my morning juice.

Of course, rather than juicing you could eat your fresh fruit and vegetables in the raw (or as close to it as possible). That offers the best benefits of all. Fruits and vegetables should be part of every meal and every snack. They are packed with fiber and antioxidants that help our body's immune system. We need them to fight off the effects of environmental pollutants. Usually the most colorful combination of fruits and vegetables contains the most nutrients.

I'm a juicer because it's convenient, and it lets me consume more fruits and vegetables every day than I normally would. I personally *love* fruits and vegetables, but it's very difficult to consume the quantity of fruits and vegetables you need for optimum health during the day. Having a glass of fruit juice in the morning and vegetable juice in the afternoon gives me many of the nutritional benefits of eating all those fruits and vegetables. Again, you still need to eat fruits and vegetables to get the benefits of the fiber, but to get the density and variety of many essential nutrients, juicing is a great way to do it. It works for me and my family. Whatever works for you, employ that daily strategy to continue to add more fruits and vegetables to your meals and to your snacks.

4. Limit processed foods. What are processed foods? Think of them like this: Anything that's not natural or has been processed—white flour, white sugar, salt—all contribute to poor health. Do you know that the average person consumes more than 200 pounds of sugar in the desserts, sodas, candies, and other processed foods they consume each year? That's 200 pounds of sugar! That's scary, as studies have actually shown that sugar acts as fuel for cancer cells to grow. And it's obviously not helping with our obesity epidemic.

Sugar and refined foods are simple carbohydrates, because it doesn't take our body very long to break them down and process them. The more we can replace these products with complex carbohydrates such as brown rice, wholegrain breads and wholegrain pastas, the more beneficial it is to our bodies. It takes our bodies longer to break down these foods, and they don't cause an immediate rush of blood sugar and insulin into our system (which has negative health impacts for a number of reasons).

A confession? I love some processed foods. Especially oatmeal raisin cookies. But here's how I personally deal with having treats and extras that make life livable: If I'm eating healthy 80 percent of the time, I find that I can be more relaxed with the remaining 20 percent, and enjoy treats and some less healthy foods without much problem.

Of course, eating healthy 80 percent of the time is no small feat. Keeping junk food out of our house helps tremendously. If you don't keep any junk food around, you may find that it's "out of sight, out of mind." So you don't crave it. But if it's sitting on the counter, I'm going to attack it. So my wife and I try to keep a healthy kitchen. If we want to indulge in a treat, we have to leave our house to get it—and that makes it so much easier to overcome temptation in moments when I'm craving something sweet.

Again, consistency is the most important trait when it comes to eating wisely. I personally feel that if you're eating well 80 percent of the time, it's okay to indulge in some less healthy foods the other 20 percent of the time. In fact, it's positive to eat some unhealthy treats that you crave regularly so that you can keep those cravings at bay.

5. Consume lots of water. Water helps our bodies in many ways and it is an important part of a healthy, high-energy nutritional lifestyle. Our bodies are composed of more than 65 percent water. Water helps to clean our bodies and also to deliver nutrients in and out of our system. Mild daily dehydration has been associated with memory loss, so consuming enough water is also very important in our mental acuity.

How much is enough? The recommended formula for water consumption is to consume one half of your body weight in ounces every day. So if you weigh 150 pounds, you should consume 75 ounces of water per day.

Another recommendation is to drink 8 to 10 eight-ounce glasses of water per day. Some nutritionists and medical researchers now feel that this recommendation was never based on solid research, and may in fact be an unnecessary volume of water to drink every day for most people, but I personally feel that it's a helpful guideline. Most people don't drink enough water, so it's important for you to find strategies that help you consume as much water as you possibly can.

And by water, I don't mean fluids in general; I mean pure water. The more you can replace other drinks—coffee, sodas, canned juices with water—the more vibrant your body and mind will be. Also if you drink an eight-ounce glass of water before each meal it will help curb your appetite and you will actually eat less, so it's extremely important to maintain a high-energy lifestyle that you consume the appropriate amount of water each day.

6. Eat smaller meals more often. Eating five to six smaller meals and snacks per day is much healthier than the standard three large meals. Our bodies and our metabolism function better when we eat smaller meals more frequently. Large meals create a system overload, causing us to lose energy and feel sluggish. When we consume smaller, healthier meals more frequently, we allow our bodies and our digestive system to work more efficiently and also to keep nutrients flowing throughout our body.

Our biggest meal of the day should be breakfast. A study done by researchers at Vanderbilt University on overweight people found that most were breakfast-skippers. Yet just by adding breakfast to the day, the average person lost 30 percent of the weight they had put on.

While it's a cliché, breakfast truly is the most important meal of the day. If you're going to eat a big meal, breakfast is likely the best time to do it because you're going to be more active during the course of the day and you'll give your body the opportunity to digest that meal.

Unfortunately, people typically tend to make dinner their largest and unhealthiest meal of the day. Most of us are not very active after eating dinner, so eating a large meal this late in the day leads our bodies to store most of it as fat.

I recommend that you experiment with eating smaller meals more frequently, and see how it impacts your energy level. **This will take planning.** Make sure you have healthy snacks already prepared and ready to grab. This will help keep your metabolism going and avoid hunger.

Two tips to help you make eating small, frequent meals easier and more satisfying:

Eat slowly. Try to consciously think about chewing your food, and try to chew 20 to 25 times per bite. When you chew your food more thoroughly, you'll help your body digest it, you will be more satisfied, and you will tend to not eat as much. (I realize chewing every bite of food 20 to 25 times sounds a little crazy, but I've done it and found it works very well for me.)

Divide restaurant portions. They're usually too large for one person. What used to feed a family of six now feeds a family of four, and the portions that restaurants serve are truly enormous. There's enough on a plate to typically feed two people. So either share the portion, or just tell your server when ordering to divide your meal in half and put half in a to-go box, so you won't be tempted to finish the whole thing when it lands in front of you. This will not only help you control the amount of food that you're eating, but it's also more cost-effective because you'll have another meal already prepared that you can eat the next day.

7. **Use supplements wisely.** Because today's foods do not always have the appropriate level of minerals and nutrients, it helps to properly supplement your food intake with vitamins and minerals. I personally take a good multi-

vitamin along with omega oil once a day, as well as an energy powder called Greenergy. I mix it in with my fresh fruit juice and it gives me a complete boost in the morning. No need for coffee. If you want to learn more about this energy powder, please visit my website at www.VitalVisionsInc.com.

I know people who take between 20 and 30 pills in a day. I think this is foolish and unhealthy. Again, it's called supplementation because it's supposed to *supplement* a good, healthy diet. In the formula I mentioned for optimum health, 75 percent of our health is dependent upon nutrition—or the things we pass through our lips. Supplementation is just five percent of this formula, so the pills are just supposed to fill in those nutrients and minerals that we might be lacking.

Typically, people want to reverse this equation and use supplements as a crutch. They want to take pills to *replace* healthy nutrition, and to wholly compensate for the fact that they're not eating properly. Again, that just doesn't work. I'm a *big* believer in nutritional supplementation—and I only take a daily multivitamin with omega oil plus and energy powder. That should reveal a lot about the role I think supplements ought to play in maintaining health.

With that said, remember that people have differing supplementation needs, based on their individual diets, body compositions, level of health, lifestyle, genetics, and other factors. In short, everyone's bodies are different and can react differently to certain stresses and stimuli (including nutrients), so don't assume a cookie-cutter approach to supplements. What works for another person won't automatically be best for you.

To learn what does suit you best, you'll need to experiment. I recommend that you become a student of good health and make it a habit to read as much as possible about the latest information on nutritional science. Explore the Internet for the latest studies. For example, if you did this now, you will find that many physicians and researchers are recommending that people take vitamin D supplements, as well fish oil supplements for cardiac health. *But things change.* And that's why it's important to keep tabs on the latest science. Ten years ago, for example, Vitamin E was the golden supplement that received a great deal of positive press. Many doctors and researchers believed it could help improve cardiac health, possibly reduce the chances of developing Alzheimer's disease, and positively affect a host of other ailments. If you scoured the health press ten years ago, you'd find that a nutrient in tomatoes called lycopene was strongly thought to lower the incidence of prostate cancer.

That was then; it's different today. Science marches on. For both vitamin E and lycopene, further studies did not show the same promising results. Many physicians and researchers now feel differently about these two particular supplements. This is why it's important to keep your knowledge of nutritional science as up-to-date as possible. Granted, you'll never have an expert's grasp of nutritional information—but even if you did, you'd only find the experts often disagree. You can become better educated. I also recommend that you have a reputable health professional advise you on the latest research; I personally consult and recommend Dr. Michael Murray (www.doctormurray.com). He has written more than 20 books. I suggest starting with *The Encyclopedia of Natural Medicine* and his latest book, *What the Drug Companies Won't Tell You and Your Doctor Doesn't Know.*

TIPS FOR CHOOSING A HIGH-QUALITY VITAMIN

No regulating body controls what's in nutritional supplements. Many times, when you purchase inexpensive drugstore vitamins or other supplements, the labels are pure fiction. The product itself will have none of the ingredient mentioned, or far less then the dosage indicated on the label. Is that legal? Sad to say, it is. That's why you need to buy from a reputable source.

So make sure you purchase supplements from a reputable company. I recommend buying vitamins made from pharmaceutical grade materials, based on pharmaceutical grade manufacturing requirements. They are produced in FDA-approved facilities and comply with US Pharmocepia guidelines to ensure digestibility and absorption. This is referred to as "USP"; look for that designation on the label. Also look for a stamp from the NSF or ConsumerLab.com. These stamps don't ensure effectiveness, but they do prove that the manufacturer has submitted its product for testing. See my website, www.VitalVisionsInc.com, for more information.

4. Get consistent exercise.

Consistent exercise is essential to maintaining an active, high-energy lifestyle.

Exercise is the vehicle that turns your body from a fat-storing machine into a fat-burning machine. Exercise is also the vehicle that provides mental and physical energy that allows you to be as productive as you can possibly be. New studies also show that exercise helps boost endorphins and makes your neurotransmitters fire more rapidly. Getting consistent exercise will help relieve stress and anxiety, and will improve your quality of sleep. The benefits go on and on.

Simply translated, you will get a sense of well-being and actually increase your focus and mental acuity if you get consistent exercise.

WHAT KIND OF EXERCISE SHOULD I DO?

When I operated sporting goods stores, people would always ask me, "Steve, what exercise do you recommend?" And I would always respond, "Choose whatever exercise you will do on a consistent basis."

The kind of exercise that you'll do *consistently* (and that won't injure you) is the right kind of exercise for you. Whether it's walking, jogging, biking, yoga, or strength training with weights, or any one of a hundred other varieties of exercise, all deliver great benefits. You can exercise on your own, do it in a class or with a group of friends. The important thing is to get some physical activity most days of the week. You should try to exercise three to six times per week, mixing aerobic conditioning (the type of exercise that significantly elevates your heart and breathing rate, such as running) with strength and flexibility training. Of course, start slow.

There is an abundance of books, videos, and websites you can explore to discover which exercise options are best for you. Keeping up with exercise research and technology can be challenging. What's more, many trends and fads—from Tae Bo videotapes to the Wii Fit system—come and go. All have a worthwhile component, especially if they get you to *move*. There are many exercise DVDs and programs that have become quite popular, and I've seen people receive great benefits from using them.

Today, at age 56, I exercise regularly and am proud to say that I'm fit. I'm not in the best shape of my life, but I'm fit—and I've achieved and maintain that fitness by practicing and living according to the six principles I've laid out in this chapter. I run three times a week and bike at least one day per week. I also do 50 to 100 pushups per day along with other strength exercises. On my 56th birthday, I rode my bike 56 miles with my friend and fellow ironman, Chuck. Next year, I plan to ride 100 miles.

YOU'RE ALREADY IN GREAT SHAPE?

That's wonderful. You have a big head start, and a great advantage. I would estimate that less than five percent of the U.S. population is in terrific shape, so you're in select company. If you're already very physical active, eating well, getting enough quality rest and following the other principles in this chapter, I congratulate you and hope you'll use this information to reinforce your positive habits.

Also, when it comes to health and nutrition, there are always opportunities for people to learn and grow and find some additional morsel they might not have considered before. So please keep an open mind.

A fringe benefit of exercising regularly? You may find that your brain is capable of receiving its greatest inspirations while you're strengthening your body. Some of my best—and most creative—ideas come to me when I'm exercising. I always keep a digital recorder (or a pen and paper) nearby to record those ideas during my workout.

"It's what you learn after you know it all that counts."

JOHN WOODEN

5. Get proper sleep, rest and rejuvenation.

I believe most people give this principle far too little consideration.

On average, the most effective rest comes from seven to eight hours of sleep. Some people may need more, some may need less. If you find that you consistently need much more sleep, you should examine the stress level in your life, and see if you can reduce it. Research shows that people who deal with stress effectively do not need as much sleep as those who don't.

There are some basic things that you can do to help create a better sleeping environment.

- First, avoid caffeine and alcohol products for four to five hours before going to bed. Both of these substances tend to disrupt the brain from getting into the state of deep, revitalizing sleep.

- You should also avoid eating a big meal in the evening. Most health professionals recommend not eating for two to three hours before going to bed.

- If possible, it's great to take a brisk, 15-minute walk after eating that last meal to aid digestion.

- Maintain a consistent bedtime and wake time. Keeping to a routine helps.

- Try not to watch TV or the news right before you go to bed. They tend to leave negative thoughts or images that remain in your subconscious and can, oftentimes, alter your sleep. We'll talk more about getting positive mental nutrition in an upcoming chapter.

- Review your written goals (we'll also get to these in an upcoming chapter) for a few minutes right before you go to bed.

TAKE MINI-BREAKS THROUGHOUT THE DAY

When you work hard, you need to take mini-breaks so you can recover and avoid burnout. I like to take frequent breaks throughout the day during which I totally disengage on what I am working on, and give my mind a rest. Sometimes I will take a quick walk or do some exercise to get my endorphins flowing. Other times I'll pick up an article, or book—something that's totally unrelated to what I've been working on.

Giving yourself several five or ten-minute breaks during the day will help you stay focused when you are really working hard and digging deep.

TAKING TIME OFF

Even God rested on the Seventh Day. Research indicates that we need to take off at least one day per week in order to avoid burnout and remain effective in our professional and personal lives.

I recommend that you take a minimum of two weeks of vacation per year, with perhaps three to four mini vacations in between. These should be times when you are completely disengaged from work, so your mind and body have adequate time to rejuvenate. You need to be sure you schedule ample time for your mind and body to recover.

Taking time off also helps you to find time to pursue your hobbies, and to engage in those things that help you to relax. I recently had the opportunity to talk with Vince Dooley, the former head coach and athletic director for the University of Georgia. He mentioned that he has taken up gardening in his retirement because it helps him to relax.

What do you love to do that makes you relax?

6. Create a support system.

We all need a support system to help us get through difficult times, and to hold us accountable to live a healthy lifestyle. I'm talking about a proper support system that includes faith, family and friends. Money and success will *not* replace a support system. Many people find this out the hard way. I'm one of them.

As I mentioned earlier, my brother Rick and I started Trillium Health Products in 1989. Within two years, we had 225 people working for us, and had $100 million in revenue. During this growth phase, juicers were selling so quickly that we couldn't keep up with demand. In 1992, *Inc.* magazine ranked us as one of the fastest-growing privately-held companies in the United States. But while we were spending $1.5 million a month on infomercials, competitors began flooding the marketplace with inexpensive juicers. There was a glut of juicers. By 1993, consumers bought five million juicers—less than half of the 11 million units that were on the market. The result? In 1993, *Inc.* could have ranked us as one of the fastest-shrinking companies in the United States.

I learned more coming down the ladder of success than I did going up. I found out what the most important things in life are. Money is not one of them—although money sure helps when it comes to paying the bills. Far more important are your faith, your family and your friends.

Now, when I talk about friends, I'm talking about the close friends you can count on one hand. I mean those friends that are there for you in the good times and the bad, and who know everything there is to know about you. They know the very best and the very worst about you. And they're always there to support you and encourage you and love you.

When my mom passed away several years ago, I arrived at the airport ticket counter to find my two closest friends, Lowery Robinson and Brett Butler, standing there. They looked at me and said, "We've got your back. We're going with you." That didn't just happen in that moment. It happened because we spent 15 years nurturing those relationships. I have been there for those two guys in their times of need.

When you make those kinds of sincere investments in a relationship, it will pay you back. If you have two or three friends like that, you're very, very fortunate.

Importantly, we need a strong support system in place so we have people who will tell us when we're going off course—and hold us accountable for maintaining our personal integrity and our sense of purpose in the good times and in the tough times.

READY FOR THE JOURNEY?

In this chapter, I've provided you with a lot of information to help you live a healthy, high-energy lifestyle. If you're sedentary and far from fit, I hope it didn't overwhelm you. It's meant to inspire you.

Remember, we ALL have the same amount of time, and that's exactly 525,600 minutes every year. We are not guaranteed a single one of those minutes, of course.

In the forthcoming chapters, we'll talk about how to use that time as wisely and as profitably as possible. But here's the question I want you to consider as you contemplate the main points in this chapter: Are you giving your body the care and attention it needs to live everyone of those precious moments to the fullest extent? If you are not, I hope you'll rethink your approach. I hope you'll make changes.

Your energy, along with your passion and focus, will determine how much you get done in a day, a week, a month, a year, a lifetime. You cannot possibly fulfill your potential when you don't have the necessary energy and vitality to do so. You owe it to yourself to have a healthy, high-energy lifestyle. And you owe it to the ones you love and the people who depend on you to live a healthy, high-energy lifestyle.

If you don't take control of your health, who will?

If you don't do it now, then when?

CHAPTER 2

KNOW WHY

"He who has a why to live, can bear almost any how."

FRIEDRICH WILHELM NIETZSCHE

"The person who knows 'how' will always have a job. The person who knows 'why' will always be his boss."

DIANE RAVITCH

In the 2005 movie *Cinderella Man,* Russell Crowe plays the role of James J. Braddock, a boxer in the 1920s and 1930s during the Great Depression. In an era of limited opportunities, boxing was the primary means for Braddock to provide for his wife and three children, and he had several difficult years when he struggled just to survive. After a streak of bad luck, he was given a chance to make a comeback—by fighting the heavyweight champion, Max Baer—and he took full advantage of it, fighting with all he had. Yet Braddock still had moments when he faltered, when his confidence was threatened and he had to remember exactly what he was fighting for.

Have you ever had those feelings? I know I have.

During one poignant scene in the film, Braddock took a hard punch in the head and was stunned for a few seconds. His strength began to wane and he was on the verge of surrendering to his opponent. Suddenly, he saw images in his mind of his wife and children going hungry, of having no money to pay the bills, and he knew that losing wasn't an option. He gathered his strength and his will and he won the fight. Later, during a press conference, a reporter asked him what changed his streak of bad luck and made his comeback so strong? Braddock said softly, "This time I know what I'm fighting for."

"What is that?" said the reporter.

"Milk."

DO YOU KNOW WHAT YOU ARE FIGHTING FOR?

The survival of Braddock's family was a powerful motivator for him, as it would be for most of us. *Cinderella Man* was incredibly inspiring to me for many reasons, but one major thing that kept jumping out is the importance of having *something worth fighting for*. Isn't it true that a certain level of success breeds complacency, while hardship ignites a fighting spirit? Most of us are not fighting a live opponent in the ring, but our battles are still very real. Instead of fighting another man with boxing gloves, we fight against our fears, our doubts and the temptation to give up when it gets too hard. But if we have a compelling reason why we must succeed, then we will continue to fight, because giving up is simply not an option.

Think about your past failures and be honest with yourself about why you failed. Did you give up because you thought the battle was hopeless, or were those pursuits just not important enough for you?

You may still hold some unrealized dreams close to your heart. You haven't totally given up on them, but you don't have a compelling reason to take action and move forward. Consider this question: Are those unrealized dreams still worth fighting for, even if the fight takes weeks, months, or years? What's holding you back? What excuses do you hold onto?

I've been a dreamer most of my life. Somebody once asked me the difference between the people who make their dreams reality and the people who don't. I boil it down to something very simple: The people who do, do; the people who don't, don't. The people who have a dream and take action almost always have a compelling reason why they must succeed at whatever it is they're going to do.

In working with hundreds of successful people, I've found that they always have compelling reasons why they must succeed in business as well as in life. They have a desire and a passion to be the very best at what they do.

People are motivated by two things: The pursuit of pleasure or the avoidance of pain. We've all heard the saying "no pain, no gain." And you know what? Most people are not willing to pay the price. They don't have a compelling reason why they must change, why they must turn their life around, why they must get into shape or why they must follow through and pursue their dreams. Having a compelling reason why you must succeed is the big equalizer in business and in life.

SIZE DOES MATTER

When you have a bigger, more compelling reason to succeed, it will give you the competitive advantage. In the true story of *Cinderella Man*, James Braddock had a more compelling reason to win a boxing match than his famous opponent, Max Baer, and that's why he beat him for the heavyweight title. Baer was fighting for glory. Braddock was fighting for milk. He was fighting for his family's well-being.

REASONS COME FIRST, RESULTS COME SECOND

Your "why" is the engine that drives your dreams. If you have a compelling reason why you must succeed at what you do, you have a much greater likelihood of taking that desire, that dream and that passion and turning it into reality. When you come up with a compelling reason why you want to do something, you can accomplish any goal even if you're not initially sure how to do it. **When you know what you want to do and why you want to do it, the "how" part seems to naturally work itself out.**

Let me share a story about my good friend Scott Rigsby. Scott graduated from high school and took a landscaping job in rural Georgia. One day on his way to a job, Scott was sitting on the trailer behind the truck with two of his buddies. As they crossed a bridge, Scott noticed a tractor trailer coming up behind them and getting real close. When the big rig tried to pass them, it caught the trailer and flipped it over. Scott was dragged for hundreds of yards while pinned under the trailer.

Scott thought he was going to die. Miraculously, a tow truck appeared and lifted the trailer off. (To this day, Scott has not heard from the man who showed up in that tow truck, and feels it was a divine occurrence.) Scott was immediately taken to a hospital, where the doctors were forced to amputate one of his legs, and do what they could to mend his other leg, which was badly damaged. For the next 12 years, Scott went through more than 25 operations and bone grafts.

He was in constant pain and became addicted to pain killers. As he says today, he "threw himself a pity party and nobody showed up."

As he continued to deal with his pain, anger and frustration, becoming a victim of his circumstances, he grew so frustrated that he actually threw himself prostrate on the floor, and said, "God, if you will just show me what to do, if you will open the door, I'll run through it."

At that point, Scott decided that he should have his other leg amputated. After an evaluation, the doctors went ahead and removed his other leg. Six weeks later, he was up and walking, pain free, for the first time since the accident. Scott then dealt with some of the addictions that he had created—getting off of the drugs and alcohol, getting away from the "I don't care" mentality. He created a compelling reason *why* he had to change his life, and why he had to resolve to take control.

Scott put a figurative stake in the ground when he decided, "I am going to change my life." He decided that the accident happened for a reason, and that reason was to inspire him to help other people to overcome their own obstacles. Specifically, he would work with wounded vets coming back from Afghanistan and Iraq to show them what was possible in their lives. So here's what Scott said to himself: "I'm going to compete in the Hawaii Ironman Competition."

If you're unaware, that's 112 miles of cycling, 26.2 miles of running and 2.5 miles of swimming. And here's the kicker: Scott didn't own a bike, did not know how to swim, and had not run—as he puts it—"more than the .2 part of the 26.2 miles in the marathon portion of a triathlon" since his accident.

In short, he did not know *how* he was going to compete, but he had something more powerful. He knew *why* he was going to do it. He had resolve born of passion and desire.

Scott knew why he must succeed. He went out and found the best trainers in Atlanta. He found people who helped him train to be a world-class runner. He found a coach at a local high school who taught him how to swim. He found an accomplished cyclist who taught him how to ride the bike he had to borrow because he could not afford one. Nothing could stop Scott because he had a compelling reason why he must succeed.

When you step outside your comfort zone, when you take a stance, when you decide that you're going to take action and move forward to do something, when you have a clear vision of what it is you want to do, you will attract the people, you will attract the resources, you will attract the things that you need to make your business work, to make your life work, to make your marriage work, to make *whatever it is that you are striving to do* work. It has happened to me numerous times in my life, and I know it will happen for you if you just create that compelling reason *why* you must succeed.

Scott Rigsby was the first double amputee to compete in and finish the Hawaii Ironman. While everybody else was changing their clothes between events, Scott was changing his legs. He has a separate set of legs for running, biking and swimming. His whole story is told in a book he wrote titled *Unthinkable*. What a great example for all of us. I always think of Scott when I feel like I can't go on and I ask, "What's my excuse?" So let me ask you the same question. What is your excuse? Let me ask you a better question. What is your reason why? Why MUST you succeed?

"By the yard, it's hard; by the inch it's a cinch."

ZIG ZIGLAR

IF YOU KNOW THE WHY, THE HOW WILL WORK ITSELF OUT

In the early 1960s, President John F. Kennedy challenged Americans to send a man to the moon by the end of the decade. Even though the technology to do that didn't yet exist, there was a compelling reason to do it: The Russians were developing a space program and had won the early stages of the space race. Kennedy wanted to make sure America kept the upper hand. He knew what he wanted to do, he just didn't know how. You know the end of the story—the U.S. made it to the moon first. Although it took tireless effort from thousands of dedicated people, the how took care of itself.

Remember the story about my father-in-law, George Soos? While recovering from triple bypass surgery, he said to me, "Steven, I don't know if I should have let them operate on me. I should have let God take me." I told him that we still needed him in our lives, and that he was still a mentor and an inspiration to me, someone who I looked up to and still needed after I lost my dad. As we talked about it, George began to create that compelling reason *why* he needed to recover and he became motivated again.

For George, it started out slowly. It usually does for everyone. You don't go from where you are to success overnight. George started with five minutes a day on an exercise bike, thinking, I need to be here for my wife and children and grandchildren. I'm going to pedal a little harder and a little faster. I'm going to keep doing this. I'm going to get up and do a little bit each day."

When you break it down, little by little, when you know what it is you want to do and you have that compelling reason *why*, it will motivate you and help you build confidence. My father-in-law continued to work out: Five minutes became 10 minutes, 10 minutes went to 15 minutes, and so on. In less than a year, George went from over 260 pounds down to 200.

When you understand why you must do something, why you must take a stand, why you must change your life, your habits, and your focus, **amazing things start to happen.**

OBSTACLES AND PAST FAILURES ARE MADE TO BE OVERCOME

I have four smart, hardworking children, three girls and a boy. Time and time again, they've shown me how the principles in this book can be applied to move through obstacles.

Take my son, Matthew. He was an All-State soccer player and an All-City football player at Westminster High School in Atlanta, Georgia. I vividly remember when he was playing in the quarterfinal game of the state football playoffs during his senior year. If his team didn't win, this would be the final football game he'd ever play in high school.

Matthew was the placekicker, the punter and wide receiver. In other words, he was out on the field for just about the whole game. His team was playing a team they'd beaten earlier in the year, and with 1:50 left on the clock, Matthew caught a pass and the safety came up and nailed him in the back. The ball was now on the 32 yard line, and Matthew's team trailed by two points, 16-14. The coach sent the field goal team out on the field. Not in top condition, either, as the holder had earlier injured his shoulder so badly he could hardly lift it above his head. It was a misty, rainy evening and the field was soggy and slick. The boys were tired from playing their hearts out for the entire game.

Being the parent of a kicker is probably the most gut-wrenching experience, other than actually being the kicker. There were more than 10,000 frenzied people in the stands. Matthew lined up for the kick, the ball was snapped, Matthew kicked and…the ball hit the upright and bounced out. No good. I can still feel his pain to this day. After the game, his coach said to him, "Matthew, you didn't lose the game for us. There were many other opportunities for us to win this game. You just lost a chance to be the hero." I walked over to my son, wrapped my arms around him and said, "Son, you were my hero, you always will be."

About three days passed before I asked Matthew how he was feeling. He said, "Dad, you think I'm going to end my career by missing a field goal in the playoff game? No way. I want to redeem myself and play in college."

Unbelievable! He had a compelling reason *why* he wanted to move beyond that missed attempt. Sure enough, he went to Furman University in Greenville, South Carolina, and walked on the football team as a freshman. He watched from the sidelines for most of his first three seasons behind a superb kicker. In his senior year, after the other fellow finally graduated, Matthew got to be the starting kicker and went on to become the Special Teams Player of the Week against Clemson University in front of 85,000 people. He did well enough (Matthew was chosen the Southern Conference Special Teams Player of the Week several times) that they actually asked him to come back for a fifth year, after he graduated on a full scholarship.

Your past does not equal your future when you have a compelling reason why you must succeed and why you must take action.

A COMPELLING REASON SUSTAINS MOMENTUM

My youngest daughter, Whitney, is a medical student at the University of Tennessee. She was about three-quarters of the way through her second year when she called me and said, "Dad, we're studying for medical school, which is 24/7. We're studying for the boards that we have to take in order to go to the next level. Everybody is burned out and ready to give up and I need you to come and talk to our class."

I went in and spoke to the medical class of about 200 students. I showed a PowerPoint slide that had a photo of an acceptance envelope from the University of Tennessee Medical School. "How did it make you feel when you received that? What were you feeling? What were you thinking?" I asked. For some of the students, the envelope meant the realization of a dream come true, proof all their hard work and energy had paid off. For others, it was the realization that they didn't get into the school that they wanted.

Then I showed a slide that had a photo of their "White Coat Ceremony." At the University of Tennessee Medical School, the very first thing they do upon beginning school is present new students with the white coat they'll wear when they graduate and become a doctor.

"Why did you want wear that white coat?" I asked. I listened to about five or six different answers—prestige, money, parents wanted me to—but none had anything to do with a compelling reason why. Finally someone said, "To help people."

I reminded them of what they felt when they first realized they wanted to be doctors, what they were really fighting for. They needed to look back and hang on to that emotion, that compelling reason. When you have that compelling reason why, it'll get you through medical school, it'll get you through the boards, it'll get you through make-up tests, and it'll help you through the process and prevent you from burning out.

I speak professionally quite a lot, and I get a lot of emails from audience members. Never have I received such a volume of heartfelt emails as I got after I spoke to those medical students. Even their professors wrote to me. Here is an excerpt from what I received:

> *"You know, we're all on the verge of burnout and I can't tell you how timely, appropriate, uplifting and motivating your presentation was. Thank you for reminding us why we wanted to become doctors. And will you come back and do it every year?"*

If your why isn't big enough, your what won't matter. Knowing why will carry you through any short-term obstacles and give you the motivation to keep moving towards your dream. What are you fighting for? If you cannot answer that question, take time right now to figure it out. Why MUST you succeed at what you are trying to accomplish? Come up with a paragraph for each goal or dream that you have. Remember, reasons come before results.

CHAPTER 3

LIVE WITH INTENTIONALITY

"Twenty years from now you will be more disappointed by the things you didn't do than by the ones you did do. So throw off the bowlines. Sail away from safe harbor. Catch the trade winds in your sails. Explore...Dream...Discover."

MARK TWAIN

When I conduct my workshops, I sometimes have the participants do an exercise in which they break up into small groups of five or six. Then I give each group an unassembled jigsaw puzzle with several hundred pieces, and I have them lay the pieces out in front of them on a desk. I give them about five minutes to put as many pieces of the puzzle together as possible. There are no rules; they can do whatever they need to do to make it happen—but they can only work with what they have right in front of them. At the end, I give a prize to the group that assembles the most pieces of their jigsaw puzzle.

Everyone struggles when they do this. Why? Because they don't have a clear picture of what the end results should look like. And that is exactly the same as going through life without a clear picture of what we want to accomplish; it's like having thousands of pieces of a puzzle but no clear view of the result we're hoping to assemble, and no clear plan of how to put them together.

During some of these workshops, I give the groups the cover of their puzzle box (showing the finished puzzle) to use as a reference. When they have a clear picture of the goal they're going for, and are able to continually look at what the end result should be, they increase their productivity three to five times. In other words, they can put the puzzle together much quicker than if they tried to figure it out on their own, without using the assembled puzzle as a visual reference.

There are some other ways in which the unassembled puzzle is a metaphor for most people's lives. It's been said that the average person has up to 64,000 thoughts per day. I've never counted mine, but I bet this number isn't far off. Now, those thoughts are actually like pieces of a puzzle. And if they're just randomly floating in our brains, they're of limited use to us. It is very difficult for us to figure out which pieces of the puzzle to take and fit together and how to complete the picture that we want to pursue.

Again, if we don't have a clear picture of what we want to *do* with all those thoughts that are floating around in our mind, our mind becomes a jumble of mini-images, all of which are nonsensical because they are incomplete. And the puzzle pieces constantly change.

If we don't intentionally try to use the thoughts we have in a productive manner, *to make progress toward a goal we value,* the randomness of life will take over. We will spend our life reacting to events and circumstances as they happen, rather than actively pursuing the life of our dreams. We will have less impact on those who depend on us and on those we come in contact with, because—in living a life *without intentionality*—we react to things as they happen rather than *proactively pursuing the things we want to attain in life.*

I spent a good deal of my life in just this way, as I've already mentioned. Through my high school and college years, and well into adulthood, I lacked a clear vision, and did not have a clear goal of how the random puzzle pieces floating around in my head—and in many aspects of my life—could ever come together to make some useful and satisfying whole. I wasn't aware of the need to have goals, so I was left to react to life as it happened rather than pursuing my passions and my dreams.

THE POWER OF TAKING ACTION

As I look back on my life, and look back at the major mistakes and the major failures I had, those mistakes came from a lack of clarity. They came from not knowing what I wanted to do, and from reacting to situations as they came up. They came from not having a picture of the finished puzzle that I could use as a guide.

I was a strong C student in college, and I wasn't exactly the sharpest tool in the shed. I was aimless, living for pleasure, and lacked ambition for anything other than football. As an athlete, I excelled when I applied myself. Sports was the only area of my life in which I felt I had a strong degree of competence.

Without goals, I didn't know what direction to go in. I didn't know what actions to take. So I spent many years taking no action at all. I was like the sloop *Narcissus*, floating aimlessly in the ocean, being carried wherever the wind and waves took me.

I've mentioned the letter to my family that Archie Bowes, Jr., my dad's friend and business associate, wrote just after my father passed away in 1968. It stated something that I found striking when I contemplated just how many years I spent feeling stuck. The passage I'm thinking of reads, "he was ahead of his years in anticipating the needs of his community and taking action to meet those needs." My father had vision. He had clear goals of what he wanted to do, and he took action to meet those needs.

Having a clear, defined goal is essential. But ultimately, will you take action to make that goal a reality? Of all the people who are smart enough to have specific dreams and goals, only a small percentage actually makes it happen. Why? Because most never take the necessary action.

*"Vision without action is a dream;
action without vision is a nightmare."*

JAPANESE PROVERB

It wasn't until I read that letter, 20 years after my father died, that I really began to understand the importance of having a vision and a plan of action.

Reading the letter in 1988, when I was 34 years old, made me think about what people would say about me after I had passed away. What would somebody write in a letter about *me*? If they wrote to my children and tried to state what I stood for, what I accomplished, what would they say? I thought a great deal about this.

Still today—and this might sound a little morbid—I often have these thoughts when I attend a funeral. (Don't you?) I think about who would show up at my funeral if I passed away at this point in my life. I think about who would get up and talk about me. What would they say? What type of things would I have accomplished that other people would find admirable? Or meaningless? What type of stories would people share about me? What type of legacy would I be leaving behind?

As Stephen Covey says in his book, *The Seven Habits of Highly Effective People*, "begin with the end in mind."

When we think about the end of our lives, how do we want to be remembered? How do we want people to talk about us, to think about us, to *feel* about us? What type of impact and influence did we have on those who depended on us and on the people that we came in contact with every day? How many children and grandchildren did we have? How did we make the world a little bit different or a little bit better? Did we live with purpose or did we just drift through life, letting things happen as they came to pass?

How did our lives make a difference?

Think about these questions now. What type of legacy will *you* leave behind?

The answers to all of these questions will be determined by what you do with your life, and you really have only two choices: You can leave it up to chance and react to life as it happens to you, or you can live with *intentionality* and take action to move towards the life of your dreams and create a life of success that will bless you and bless those around you.

Stick with me, and I will give you some tools to help you do that.

SETTING GOALS

A lot of people ask me, "Does setting goals really work?" They look at me skeptically, because—let's face it—they've heard a million times that you need to set goals in order to move your life in a positive direction. They've heard it so many times that it seems like an old yarn that is very easy to say, but has lost any real meaning.

When I speak to an audience, one of the first things I do is ask, "How many people here have goals?"

Recently, I did this at the beginning of a talk in Chicago. I was speaking to a group of about 300 people who worked in the sales force of an actuarial company. When I asked how many people had goals, I would say that perhaps 80 people raised their hand.

Then I asked, "How many of you have clearly defined, measurable goals that you've *written down?*"

It went down to 20 people. I counted. Twenty out of 300 people had written goals.

Finally, I asked, "How many people have clearly defined, measurable goals in more than just your business life?"

There was just one hand left. It belonged to a young man.

I had never met this young man. I had not spoken to him before my talk. Nothing about him was unusual...except that he was the only person in the room of 300 with his hand still raised.

I said, "I can tell you, based on my past experience, that I would wager the fee that I'm getting paid to speak today that you're one of the top income earners and influencers in this company."

And as it turned out, this young man was the number two revenue generator in the organization. How did I know this? I'm not psychic. It's pretty simple. Statistics show that people who have clearly defined, written, measurable goals outperform most other people. Hands down.

WANT TO OUTPERFORM 97 PERCENT OF PEOPLE?
WRITE DOWN YOUR GOALS!

Let me give you some support and validation for that statement, using a study done on the 1954 graduating class from Yale University. Researchers asked these young men the same type of question I now use in my talks: "How many of you have clearly defined, written, measurable goals?"

At the outset, researchers found that three percent of the men in Yale's class of 1954 had written goals and an action plan to achieve those goals. Researchers tracked those students over the next 20 years. What did they find? The three percent of the class that had clearly-defined, written, measurable goals out-earned the other 97 percent of the class *combined.*

Another study done at the Harvard Business School tracked the graduating class of 1979. It found that 84 percent of the class had no goals at all (other than to enjoy themselves), and 13 percent had goals and plans but they did not write them down. Like the Yale 1954 grads, only three percent of Harvard's class of 1979 had written goals and a written plan of action to complete those goals.

Ten years after graduation the Harvard class of '79 was resurveyed: The results showed that the 13 percent who had goals in their head—those who had not written their goals down but at least said they *had* goals—were earning twice as much as the other 84 percent of grads. The remaining three percent who had clearly defined, measurable goals and a *written* plan of action were earning *ten times* as much as the other 97 percent *combined.*

The point is clear: Having clearly defined, *written* goals will make you more successful. And having clearly defined, written goals with a plan of action that you review daily can make you extremely successful.

SHOULD YOU SET GOALS IN YOUR *MARRIAGE?*

Absolutely. If you set clear, long-term goals in your relationship, it will help you overcome the short-term obstacles that occur in every marriage. Marriages are particularly prone to complacency because people see no need for goals, as they often believe they can keep repeating the behaviors that worked well at one time.

For many couples, marriage is the epitome of early success. As newlyweds, and perhaps for several of the early years, partners are happy with each other. But as the marriage goes on, they hit a hiccup; bad things happen, challenges come up; opportunities that bring stress arise, and financial struggles occur. One day, partners look at each other and simply say, "I'm out of here. This is not what I signed up for." Setting long-term goals can help you avoid becoming a part of that unhappy pack. My wife and I set new goals for our marriage every year, and every 90 days set aside time to review how we are doing. We ask ourselves three questions:

1) What's working?

2) What's not working?

3) What will we do differently in the next 90 days?

IF IT'S SO DARN EASY...

If having written goals (and action plans to achieve them) is so powerfully effective, why do so few people have them?

There are several specific reasons I've identified, which I'll share with you now:

1. They're comfortable right where they are.

It's called the law of familiarity. People without goals are often comfortable with what they're doing, and comfortable in their surroundings. They don't *genuinely* wish to significantly change the state and condition of their lives.

Perhaps they eke out a somewhat satisfying living or existence by simply doing what they've always done, and they have no point of reference to compare their current lives with what they're *potentially capable of doing*—so they stay right where they are, doing exactly what they're doing. They don't set compelling goals because they don't want to move from where they are to where they *could* be.

You know several of these people. Do you feel sorry for them? Or do you envy them?

2. They're afraid of what other people might think.

I remember when I started telling the people around me that I was going to start a company with my brother, selling a machine that made juice from fruits and vegetables. They looked at me like I was from another planet. Some smirked. It wasn't pleasant.

I remember when I walked into a bank and told them that my brother and I wanted to start a company to sell "juicers" to people, to help them live a more nutritional, healthy lifestyle. I assured the bankers that people would put carrots and oranges and celery and spinach and parsley into our machines, and out would come juice that can make people healthier. Well, the loan officers weren't receptive. I went to 10 banks and everyone I met looked at me like I was crazy. Needless to say, they wouldn't lend me any money. They didn't believe in what I was doing. I'm very lucky that I didn't take it too personally and give up.

Many people are afraid to share what's deep inside their heart, what their dream is, because they fear getting this negative reaction. Perhaps they want to be a Broadway singer, or they want to ride their bike across the United States, or they want to go to Hollywood and become an actor...but they never mention it to others for fear that they will be ridiculed. So it never becomes a *real* goal. And they never take action to accomplish it.

3. They never learned how to set goals.

Even if you attended college, you probably never had formal instruction on how to set and achieve goals.

Recently, I spoke to two graduate classes at a local university in Atlanta. The students there had an abundance of knowledge but they had no idea how to set goals, or how to push themselves beyond their comfort zone, and how to take the knowledge they had and apply it in the real world.

Herbert Spencer wrote that the great aim of education is not knowledge but *action*. I can read all the books I want about good health and how to get in shape, but until I start working out and eating properly, I am not going to get into good shape.

Whatever type of knowledge you possess has to receive a dose of action to turn it into a practical application.

I've attended numerous seminars on setting goals. I've read a multitude of books and I've listened to just about every CD on setting goals. But nothing changed in my life, and nothing will change in your life, until you take the action and turn that knowledge into a plan and execute it. And move from where you are to *where you want to be.*

4. They don't realize the power and importance of goals.

I didn't grow up in a home where goal-setting and success were topics of conversation. So I wasn't exposed to it. I didn't know how powerful goals were. Then I took some courses.

I remember the very first workshop I took. It was a Dale Carnegie course. During the opening session, the instructor made us all repeat this:

"I know men in the ranks that are going to stay in the ranks. Why? I'll tell you why: Simply because they haven't the ability to get things done."

To be politically correct, today they might say, "I know men and women in the ranks that are going to stay in the ranks," but the point is the same. This made a lasting impression on me. Those in the ranks who will always stay in the ranks, and never rise above, *don't have the ability to take action.* Let me rephrase that: I believe we all have the ability, but we don't all choose to use it.

Most people "in the ranks" don't set goals. And that's a contagious bit of inaction. You tend to take on the habits and the tendencies of the people you surround yourself with. Are the people you're hanging out with high achievers? Are they goal-oriented? If they're not, then chances are you won't be setting any goals, either.

5. They've had some early success.

I see this all the time with clients. Success breeds complacency. When people have had success (especially early in their careers), and have had the experience of generating significant recognition or significant revenue, they can get caught in a cycle of working and living that doesn't evolve. They don't go forward because what they're doing had worked quite well—at some past point in their lives.

This happened to me, actually. So, I know first-hand that if you rack up some notable early success in business, you tend to stop doing the things that make up, what I call a "bootstrapping mentality." You stop doing those things that got you to that successful point, and you start relying on money. You begin to throw money at people, to try to get them to fix problems, rather than using the same creative resources and power that you used when you started your business.

You move from a "bootstrapping mentality" to what I call the "fat, dumb and happy mentality," where you just rest on your past experiences and past success. In this place, we no longer look for ways to continue to push ourselves out of our comfort zone or continue to look for ways to improve our business, health, and relationships.

6. They fear failure.

Let's not sugarcoat it: Failure can certainly be worthy of fear. I know; I've failed quite a lot. And again, I've already mentioned that failures can be very valuable lessons, as long as they don't kill you.

But people who don't set goals have usually never failed themselves, because they've never taken any risks. They have a *vicarious* fear of failure, from (an often limited or misinterpreted) exposure to someone else's experience.

In other words, people will say, "My Uncle Bob tried to start a business back in 1986 and he failed. Why should I make the same mistake?" They're afraid to step outside that little box where life is very predictable, where they feel they can't fail because they know what they need to do each day to maintain a status quo. They can't truly *succeed* at anything, but avoiding the fear of failure outweighs that negative for many people.

People get stuck in that box and are afraid to step out because they don't know what's outside of that safe environment. They don't know what's going to happen if they leave their box, and they won't act unless they can be certain of the outcome. Their "mind monsters" offer many good excuses why they must never get out of the box: *What would happen if you failed? Would people think of you as a failure? Could you live with yourself if you failed?*

Here's the truth: If you haven't failed, then you really haven't lived up to your potential, because you haven't attempted anything significant enough that pushes you outside of your comfort level.

"Just do it."

NIKE

I remember when I first saw Nike's famous "Just do it" ad in 1992, in *Sports Illustrated*. Here's how the ad copy went:

Too often we are scared, scared of what we might not be able to do, scared of what people might think if we tried. We let our fear stand in the way of our hopes. We say 'no' when we want to say 'yes'; we sit quietly when we want to scream, and we shout with the others when we should keep our mouths shut. Why? After all, we only do go around once. There's really no time to be afraid. So stop. Try something you've never tried before. Risk it. Enter a triathlon; write a letter to the editor; demand a raise; call winners at the toughest court; throw away your television; bicycle across the United States; try bobsledding; try anything.

Speak out against the designated hitter; travel to a country where you don't speak the language; patent something; call her; call him. You have nothing to lose and everything, everything, everything to gain. Just do it.

That was one of the most compelling advertisements I had ever seen. It still is.

The concepts apply to you and to me. If we don't step out of our comfort zone, if we don't get beyond our fears, we won't accomplish anything close to what we could if we just took that first step.

So, let's talk seriously about failure. Almost every batter in baseball's Hall of Fame, from Babe Ruth to Hank Aaron, failed 70 percent of the time. But they succeeded at least 30 percent of the time, and it put them in the Hall of Fame. It made them famous. Whatever we do, we all have to step up to the plate of life and accept that we must fail at some point in order to learn how to succeed.

How much have I failed? Well, I've been involved in 17 different businesses and I have failed at most of them. But those failures became the building blocks of the greatest success that I have ever had.

Remember, failing is part of the process of gaining wisdom.

LIFE IS A SERIES OF NON-FATAL MISTAKES

If a mistake doesn't kill you, and you learn from it, it's not a mistake at all; it's part of the process of gaining wisdom and learning what to do next time around. And that's true in business and life.

The only thing that constitutes true failure is if you get knocked down and don't get back up and try again. That is the only true failure in life.

*"Success is not final, failure is not fatal. It is
the courage to continue that counts."*

WINSTON CHURCHILL

7. They fear success.

Yes, you read that right. Some people don't set goals because they think, "What happens if I *succeed*?" Will I create a new standard that I can't live up to long-term? Will people expect me to *always* succeed? Will people resent me? Will it change my relationship with my partner? Success brings responsibility—what if I can't ultimately live up to it?"

Many people feel these fears are quite legitimate. But few people answer them honestly when they contemplate them. Instead, sour grapes come into play. People will say, "Well, people who succeed in my profession have a lot of money, and their lives just become a disaster because money ruins them."

For the record, money is not the root of all evil; it's the *love* of money that you need to watch out for. But if your motives are sound, you can generate income and use that to create a life for yourself and your family that will not only benefit you, but also benefit others. Your success will bless others. The more successful you become, the more you can benefit the people in your world, and the more you can contribute to making the world a better place.

Many people know this intrinsically; they just insist on believing the opposite because it allows them to think that they have a plausible rationale for not even trying to achieve the success they could very likely attain. It's "choosing to lose." It's sour grapes, plain and simple.

"Success corrupts, power corrupts," some will say, shaking their heads. If you truly believe that, then why not be a solution to the problem? Set compelling goals and come up with compelling reasons to achieve them, and then let your success make a difference to your family, your community, and the world. I'll say it again; your success truly will bless other people, if you make it so.

Nelson Mandela expressed it beautifully:

> "Our deepest fear is not that we are inadequate. Our deepest fear is that we are powerful beyond measure. It is our light, not our darkness that most frightens us. We ask ourselves, 'Who am I to be brilliant, gorgeous, talented, fabulous?' Actually, who are you not to be? You are a child of God. Your playing small does not serve the world. There is nothing enlightened about shrinking so that other people won't feel insecure around you. We are all meant to shine, as children do. We were born to make manifest the glory of God that is within us. It's not just in some of us; it's in everyone. And as we let our own light shine, we unconsciously give other people permission to do the same. As we are liberated from our own fear, our presence automatically liberates others."

THE TOP 10 REASONS TO ESTABLISH WRITTEN GOALS

Now that you have a firm idea why people don't create goals, here are the reasons why you should take the time—today, or this week—to create written goals. Some we've already alluded to earlier in this chapter, but they are worth repeating.

Here's what you gain by clearly defining your goals and writing them down:

1. You keep your life in better balance, as you proactively and intentionally determine how you will use your time and energy.

I've worked with thousands of people and hundreds of couples over the years, and when I ask, "What is your greatest challenge?" the number one answer—99 times out of 100—is, "How do I balance work and family?"

That is the great challenge that most people face. Most households are dual income earners now; the husband and the wife are both working. People spend an inordinate amount of time at work. And people think, "Well if I could own my own business and be my own boss then I would have more freedom and more time."

But the reality is when you own your own business—and I've been there—you spend a lot of time thinking, "I don't know if I own the business or if the business owns me." When you own the business, you're involved with it 24/7. It's easy to become obsessed. So your business temporarily thrives, but your husband leaves you. When you have clearly defined, written, measurable goals in *all* areas of your life, it creates the balance and harmony to dictate where you spend your time and energy. "Sundays are work-free, and only to be spent with my wife and my children," is a pretty clear goal. And you'll know when you're violating it.

Again, remember the statistics: People who have clearly defined, measurable, *written* goals in all areas of their life outperform the masses combined. So come up with those clearly defined goals in every area of your life.

2. Your goals serve as a GPS to guide you through life with intentionality, instead of just letting life happen to you. Remember my adventure on the sloop *Narcissus* in the introduction of this book? That's what "no written goals" looks like. Instead of just drifting, having written goals will give you a long-term perspective, which will help you to overcome short-term obstacles.

Most of the mistakes I've made in my life were made in the heat of the moment. I had a short-term perspective, was just looking at the circumstances. When I fall back into that kind of knee-jerk behavior, my wife Indy has a great saying to help me regain perspective. She says, "The story's not finished yet."

By taking the time to write down your goals, you automatically move into a long-term perspective. You remember what it is you're trying to accomplish, and you remember who it is you're trying to become. Then, when short-term obstacles pop up, you can respond according to your spelled-out life goals, rather than reacting in the moment on your emotions, or reacting by asking, "Well, what would everybody else do?" A much better question to ask in those moments is: "Given the person I want to become and what I want to accomplish, what is the wise thing to do in this situation?" And respond to *that* question, rather than reacting to the situation.

3. Your goals tell your brain what to focus on and what to think about. Remember all those puzzle pieces? When you have written goals, you have clarity on what the final picture should look like. And that helps put those 64,000 daily thoughts into some useful order.

Men may have a greater challenge in this category. Of those 64,000 thoughts that we have, up to 60,000 of them are about one thing (do I really need to tell you what it is?). So we have to work a little harder to really make sure that we're focused on what we want to accomplish, and to write those goals down, so we tell our brain what to focus on and what to think about. Left to its own agenda, it certainly knows how to amuse itself.

4. You build self-confidence as you take action and begin accomplishing goals. The following is a personal example. When I wrote down my goal for running a road race, I stated it like this: "It is July 4, 1986 and I just ran the Peachtree Roadrace (10K) in less than 40 minutes."

A 10K is a 6.2-mile race. Running it in under 40 minutes is a challenging goal for someone who's not a dedicated, everyday runner. To achieve this goal, I found a running expert and asked him, "What do I need to do in order to run a sub-40 10K? I have four months to train."

This expert was an All-American track runner in college, and he developed an action plan for me that had many smaller, specific goals. And I wrote each of those specific goals down. Accomplishing each small goal gave me the confidence to tackle the next one, and they grew progressively more difficult.

Running 6.2 miles in under 40 minutes breaks down to math. You need to maintain a pace that's well under a seven minute mile. At first, I needed to build endurance and speed. I needed to be able to run a quarter mile in less than 1.5 minutes, and then run a half-mile in under three minutes, and then run a mile in under six minutes. As I followed the action plan, my runs became longer, stretching from two miles to four, then to six and eight. By the end of my four-month training regimen, I was on course to achieve my goal and running a sub 40-minute 10K race.

I finished the 10K in 38 minutes and 47 seconds. I didn't have a clue how I was going to do it when I started; I could barely run a half-mile. But I accomplished this personally meaningful goal by following a plan that you can use for any goal:

1. I decided what I wanted to do and produced a clear, defined WRITTEN goal.

2. I enlisted an expert's help to develop a plan of action.

3. I created specific mini goals, which I wrote down.

4. I tackled each small goal, building up confidence and increasing my ability slowly.

5. I celebrated when I reached my goal. Celebrating is important.

5. You know with assurance when to say "yes" and when to say "no." When you don't have clearly defined, written goals, every opportunity can seem worth taking, or not worth taking. How can you tell? What is the gauge you use to determine whether you want to move toward something or away from something?

For example, my daughter Stefany had a clear, defined goal regarding the job that she wanted. She specifically wanted to work for a small boutique public relations firm that specialized in promoting products. She worked in PR in New York, and was leaving the job because it didn't fit her goal. She didn't have another job, and there was an economic crisis going on. Many people were looking for work, and many employers were laying people off.

As parents, Indy and I were a little nervous about her plans.

During the four months she spent searching for a job, Stefany continued to have a clear vision of the position that she wanted. She received three job offers during those four months, and turned them all down. They weren't specifically what she was looking for.

I started becoming more nervous. I'm the one who tells everyone to *bypass the good to get to the great*, but I said, "Stefany, people are being laid off; many companies aren't hiring, and you've had three opportunities to go to work and you haven't accepted them. Why?"

She said, "Dad, it's not what I want to do. I know the opportunity I want is out there, and I know I'm going to find it. I have to give up these good opportunities to find the best opportunity for me. I am just following your advice."

OUCH!

Three weeks later, she found the position that was exactly what she had envisioned. It was a perfect example of living with intentionality and sticking to clearly defined, written goals. If you do this, you'll know when to say "yes," and you won't be afraid that you're settling—whether it's in your career, relationship, or any aspect of your life.

6. You have a powerful source of intrinsic motivation. You won't need to rely on something or someone else to get yourself fired up and inspired. I spent most of my time in that camp, needing somebody to tell me what to do, or needing a coach to get me excited.

But the people who are most excited in life, and have the greatest influence and impact in life, are intrinsically motivated. They are *motivated internally* to do the things that they wish to do. And typically it's because they create written, compelling goals that inspire them to move in a set direction, to move outside their comfort zone, even though they might not know how to do it at first.

"Do not let what you cannot do interfere with what you can do."

JOHN WOODEN

John Wooden was someone I admired greatly. He was the only basketball coach inducted into the Basketball Hall of Fame who was also inducted as a player. His teams recorded seven straight NCAA championships, from 1967 to 1973. Between 1971 and 1974, UCLA won 88 consecutive games, a college basketball record. John Wooden not only cared about winning, but he cared even more about how he won.

A surprising fact? For the first 16 years he was at UCLA, he didn't win championships. He even had a losing record for some of that time. But he had compelling goals, and he always had his players establish compelling goals. For 16 years he persevered with a plan, grooming people to buy into his plan. He had a dream; he had a vision.

He set college basketball records that many believe will never be surpassed. Here's what's really ironic: If John Wooden were coaching today at a Division One school with a losing record, they would likely fire him after the first two or three years. Allow him to remain the coach without winning any tournaments or events for 16 years? That would be unthinkable today.

7. **You have a means of correcting your course to arrive at your destination.** Remember the *Narcissus*, heading for the Bahamas? When we were adrift at sea, we had to readjust our course. And we changed our goal from going to the Bahamas to just getting back to land. Similarly, if Stefany had been searching for work for 15 months without finding her dream job, instead of five, she might have had to change her course. This isn't settling for second best, or reacting to circumstances of the moment; it's adjusting your course in a very purposeful way when it's necessary to do so.

Businesses have to do this all the time, though some will stubbornly stick to obsolete goals far too long, even when it's obvious they should change course.

To get to the heart of this, I always ask clients to answer three questions honestly:

1. *What's working?* What's working in your business? What's working in your life? What's working in your marriage?

2. *What's not working?* What's not working in those same areas? As you take inventory of what's working and what's not working, it allows you to do the most important thing: Sit down and make a course correction.

3. *What are you going to do differently in the next 90 days to help correct what's not working?* Write down those goals!

8. You attract the resources and people you need to achieve your goals. It's called the law of attraction: The more clarity you have, and the more you can write down and visualize what it is you want to happen, the better able you are to attract the things that *you want to attract* in your life.

When we started Trillium Health Products, we knew what we wanted to do and we knew why we wanted to do it. The goal was to build a $50 million company in five years. As for the *why*, once again, I didn't want anybody to ever feel like I did when I lost my dad. I wanted to educate people about good health and proper nutrition so they could take care of themselves and live a healthy lifestyle, in part for the sake of their families and children.

As for *how* we were going to do it? We had no clue. But, with a lot of hard work, the how part naturally worked itself out.

IF YOU ALREADY KNOW HOW TO ACCOMPLISH A GOAL, IS IT REALLY WORTH PURSUING?

To sum it up, when you know *what* you want to do, and you have a compelling reason why you want to do it, the *how* part will naturally work itself out. You will attract resources and people you need to make it happen.

My advice? Always go big. **Little goals and little visions will attract little thinkers and little resources. Big goals and big visions will attract big thinking people and big resources.**

My oldest daughter, Courtney, demonstrated this principle when she graduated from high school. Courtney, a brilliant student, applied to six high-caliber schools. Her backup school was Vanderbilt University in Nashville, Tennessee. She was told that getting into the other schools would be a challenge because they are very competitive with their acceptances. The only school that accepted her was Vanderbilt, so she consulted with us and her high school counselor on what she should do.

The counselor told her to go to Vanderbilt, get straight A's and to transfer to an Ivy League school (if she still desired to do so) in her sophomore year. This still wouldn't be easy, as Ivy League schools only take about 10 percent of their total enrollment as transfer students. So what did Courtney do? She pursued her dream goal and got straight A's her freshman year (I told you she was brilliant), and then applied to two Ivy League schools and Georgetown University. She was accepted by all of the schools, and chose to enroll at Columbia University for the next three years of her college experience. She was able to study abroad and even graduated a semester early.

Don't settle, go for your dream, and "If at first you don't succeed, adjust your plans and try, try again."

Remember, **goals change everything**. They tell your brain what to focus on and what to think about. When you move from a goal that you know how to accomplish to one you don't know how to accomplish it makes your brain think in a manner it normally wouldn't. And it's the same for you: If you set little goals that you know how to accomplish and you never fail, you won't ever learn what you're really capable of.

9. Your goal-building helps you create the future in advance. I have six pictures that represent a goal for every area of my life. I'm looking at them now. It's the picture of what I want to do, and of what I want to be in the future.

Actually, the writing of this book is a result of putting it on my visual goal map, as a daily reminder of what I'm trying to accomplish.

Here's the way it works: **The pictures you create in your head turn into the reality you hold in your hand.** Anything that was ever accomplished in this world—the greatest athletic feats, the greatest scientific feats, the greatest romances, the greatest achievements—all started as an idea or a vision or a dream in somebody's mind. And they didn't happen until they were written down and somebody took action to make them happen.

This is me with Scott Rigsby, The Ironman (whose story is told on pg. 55-57) after a 46 mile bike ride to raise money for The Scott Rigsby Foundation. I look at this daily as a visual reminder for my fitness goal and also for inspiration.

"Imperfect action is always better than perfect inaction."

HARRY TRUMAN

10. You stay on the offensive. Playing life to win is playing offense, not defense. Playing defense is playing not to lose. I meet so many people who play life not to lose. They play defense; they protect themselves, they live in a sheltered world where they don't step out to see what they're really capable of doing.

I've found that many business people in our volatile economy are stuck in their businesses because they're playing defense, and trying to protect themselves from not losing, rather than playing offense and being creative and taking action to make their product or service more relevant in the current environment.

The people who are creative and make their product or service more relevant in this marketplace are the ones who are thriving. Remember, almost 70 percent of the current Fortune 500 companies were started in a down economy.

When you play offense, you take control. In sports, a good offense really is your best defense. In the last 15 years, teams with offenses ranked in the top five have won more Super Bowls than teams with top-five defenses. Offense is where it's at. It's making something happen, being creative, moving forward and—above all—taking action.

When you stand up and take action, good things begin to happen.

HOW TO WRITE EFFECTIVE GOALS

So, how do you actually write an effective, clearly defined goal? The SMART acronym is a simple and useful way to break it down.

Specific: Highly effective goals should be written and specific. If a goal is not written down, and you merely keep it in mind, it does not have the same power as a written goal. **WRITE IT DOWN, MAKE IT HAPPEN.** When you write it down make sure it is specific and well defined. Instead of saying: "I want to lose weight," say, "I weigh 180 pounds and my body fat is less than 20 percent." Instead of saying, "I want to make more money," say, "I make $150,000 a year." Your written goal should stretch you beyond your comfort zone.

Measurable: Highly effective goals are measurable. If you can't measure your goal, how will you know when you achieve it? Let me give you an example. If your goal is stated as, "I will improve my relationship with my wife," how will you know if you accomplish it? Instead, if you say, "I improved my relationship with my wife by reading three relationship books this month," then you will, at the very least, have something to measure. Your goals should also be meaningful to you and motivate you to move toward them. Remember, you must have a compelling reason why you want to achieve a goal. The best way to keep a commitment, to reach a goal, is to understand *why* you are striving for it.

Action-oriented: Highly effective goals are stated positively and in the present tense, as if you have already accomplished the goal. This moves you towards action. You should have an action step for each of your goals; you need to compile the details, make a plan, and write down all of the required activities. Prioritize and time-organize them, and rewrite them as often as necessary to make your plan effective. Revise your list of goals, improve it, plan it...but most importantly, put it on paper.

Realistic: Highly effective goals need to be realistic and relevant to you. They need to be achievable. Make an assessment of available resources, knowledge and time. Taking an action-oriented mindset will attract people and resources that aren't initially visible—you can and should factor this in. Just make sure you aren't confusing achievements with miracles. For example, I could state a goal of wanting to become a professional football player, but I don't think the NFL is looking for a 56 year-old tight end right now. This is just not in the scope of my resources.

Time-based: Highly-effective goals are time-bound. Deadlines put positive pressure on you to take action; otherwise it's just human nature to keep putting things off. Strangely enough, we tend to procrastinate on goals that are the most valuable to our long-term success.

To put it all together, here is an example of a written goal that hits all of the above points:

I weigh 180 pounds and my body fat is less than 20 percent by December 31, 2012.

Now I have a goal that is Specific, Measurable, Action-oriented, Realistic and Time-based. That seems SMART to me!

TAKING ACTION, TAKING RESPONSIBILITY

One of my favorite anecdotes about taking action concerns a good friend and client, Bill Bartmann. You may have seen his name on *Inc.* magazine's list of the "25th Wealthiest Men that Nobody Ever Knew About." Bill started a business back in the 1980s with a $13,000 loan.

He sat down with his wife and wrote his idea down on a napkin. Seven years later he had a $3 billion dollar company.

In 2008, Bill and I were working together at a "Get Motivated" event in Roanoke, Virginia, before an audience of about 10,000 people. We were scheduled to zip off to the airport to catch our departing flight, right after the presentation.

Naturally, as we got out to the parking lot, everybody was leaving at the same time. There was complete gridlock. No one was moving. We knew if we sat there much longer, we were going to miss our flight.

Suddenly, Bill jumped out of the car and disappeared into the crowd of people and autos. About five minutes later, cars started moving. As we got closer to the exit of the parking lot, we could see Bill standing in the middle of the bottleneck point, directing traffic! He was the picture of calm authority, pointing, waving and signaling to each driver. In 10 minutes, we were out of the parking lot and speeding to the airport. We made that flight with time to spare.

I guess that's why he's a billionaire, I remember thinking. He didn't let circumstances dictate his fate. He got up and took action. He took responsibility. You can't do one without the other. When he took action, he took responsibility for changing the circumstances that 10,000 people found themselves in. And when he took that responsibility, he had to make something positive happen.

Many people are stuck in their own gridlock; letting circumstances (or their *perceptions* of their circumstances) dictate what happens to them. They sit there and wait for something to change instead of taking action.

Nothing happens until you take action.

ACT ON WHAT YOU <u>ALREADY</u> KNOW

Here's a rule of the action-based life that took me a long time to learn: Stop asking or praying for wisdom and take action based on what you *already* know. For example, most of us already know that smoking cigarettes will increase our chances of getting cancer and heart disease. For my part, I *already* know that if I don't invest time and effort and energy with my wife and children, those relationships will falter. I already know that if I sit down and eat a pint of ice cream before I go to bed every night, it is not going to be good for my health. I know that if I don't get out and network with the right people every day, my business is not going to have an opportunity to grow.

PRAYER HELPS, BUT ACTIONS ALWAYS CREATE RESULTS

I remember when I first learned how to pray. It was really uncomfortable. My prayers usually sounded something like this: "Dear God, gimme, gimme, gimme, help me, help me, help me." The focus was totally on me.

And as I grew in my faith, I started to pray more for others. I might say, "God, please help the Smith family, the Jones family. Please help the people in Haiti who went through the earthquake." The focus went onto other people.

As I continued to grow, it went into the third phase. Instead of just praying, I took action.

When you hear about somebody that is in need, instead of just praying for them, take action. In my opinion, God always works through other people. The earthquake victims in Haiti didn't receive help until others took action. It's the same way in your local community or in your own small circle of influence. Prayer works, but actions always create results. So pray as if everything depends on God, and work as if everything depends on you.

Goals + Action = Change. The actions we take today will start to change the outcome of what happens tomorrow. And the more you can crystallize your goals into a form that makes them real and tangible, the more compelling they will be. And the better able you will be to achieve them.

What action do you need to take right now that will move you one step closer to one of your goals? Don't wait. Do it now.

You'll find more exercises and tools to help you set effective goals at my website, www.VitalVisionsInc.com.

CHAPTER 4:

FIND YOUR GENIUS

"Don't ask yourself what the world needs; ask yourself what makes you come alive. And then go and do that. Because what the world needs is people who have come alive."

HAROLD WHITMAN

"Follow your passion, and success will follow you."

ARTHUR BUDDHOLD

You have no greater responsibility than to determine what you are meant to accomplish on this earth. Why do you exist?

As human beings we need a sense of purpose in our lives as much as we need food, water and oxygen. This sense of purpose provides meaning and significance to our lives. It makes us feel useful, and is a constant reminder that "my life matters." With a deep sense of purpose or mission, you live from the inside out. You become the force that triggers your actions. Your outer life honestly and accurately reflects your inner life—your values, priorities and principles. You begin living authentically, behaving more freely and intuitively. When you tap into your personal mission, you become more creative, energetic and passionate. Like a child at play, you become totally absorbed in the pursuit of your goals because your goals are in sync with what you're all about.

> *"According to the depth of which you draw your life,*
> *such is the depth of your accomplishment."*
>
> RALPH WALDO EMERSON

Without a deep sense of purpose, life is empty and devoid of true significance or long-term meaning. This type of existence is characterized by cynicism, pessimism, apathy and, ultimately, a life of mediocrity where you go through the motions in perpetual survival mode.

The 1981 movie *Chariots of Fire* offers some vivid illustrations of a life lived with purpose. Two scenes in particular stand out to me. In the first, Harold Abram is on a training table, getting ready to run the race of his life: The 100-yard dash in the Olympics. He says, "I am 24 years old, I am constantly in pursuit, and I don't even know what it is that I am chasing."

Without purpose our lives seem unfulfilled, uncontrollable and tiresome. Contrast that scene with another, in which Eric Liddell says to his sister, "Jenny, I believe God made me for a purpose, the mission fields of China. But he also made me fast. And when I run I feel His pleasure."

When do you feel God's pleasure?

There are four benefits to knowing your life's purpose: It will give you focus, it will simplify your life because you stay focused on the things that matter and delete everything else, it will increase your motivation in life because you'll have a clear direction, and it will give meaning to your life.

If you recall the letter my father's friend wrote to my family after my dad had passed away, it stated, "Your dad was ahead of his time in anticipating the needs of others and taking action to meet those needs. He was a counselor and a friend to those who were lost or stumbled. He had personal magic, and gave a lift and brought a smile to those he met each day. In the eyes of God and the eyes of man, your dad lived a successful life."

To me, that illustrates a life lived with purpose and clarity. Even though I didn't know this about my dad, other people saw him as having an evident sense of purpose. We all share a common purpose of learning and growing, but within that larger purpose we must find our genius.

Your genius is your unique path to learning, growing and contributing to the world. No matter how far you stray from your genius it is always waiting for you, because no one but you can fulfill it. Every life experience, no matter how random it may seem, can be utilized to your advantage. It can fuel your genius. As I like to say, everything you have experienced in life has prepared you for what you're about to do. When you arrive at your genius, you will know it.

A sense of destiny will come over you as you come to understand the difference in the world that only you are equipped to make. The more you experience your genius, the more you will be drawn into it. Tinges of dissatisfaction will fade. You will enjoy invigorating surges of self-worth as you let go of the need to compare yourself with others. You will be healthier, more prosperous and full of joy.

We spend a lot of our lives wishing we could "act like him," or "look like her," or "be as successful as him." When you unlock your genius, however, your sense of purpose and passion sweeps away your desire for what somebody else has. We each have many different potential paths in life, but we have only one genius.

They say "perfect is the enemy of the good," meaning we should go ahead with a small, useful action instead of waiting for some absolutely ideal solution. There's logic in that, but I feel we must often bypass things that are merely good in order to reach what is truly great. Developing your genius is all about this: God had one purpose when He made you. You came into this life with a unique vision or dream. For some this dream will shake the entire world and for others it will soothe just one tiny home. In either case the world is left a better place.

Sooner or later, we are all confronted with the internal question of whether we are heeding our call and following our ultimate vision.

"Don't measure yourself by what you have accomplished, but by what you should have accomplished with your ability."

JOHN WOODEN

We each have a unique gift and purpose. Our job is to find it and use it to the best of our ability. Throughout your life you will constantly change and become slightly or extensively different from the previous version of yourself. With each change you will move closer or slip farther from your genius. Most people consider change to be an external event that occurs randomly and haphazardly. We react to life as if it happens like a leaf in a windstorm. This causes us to be thrown off course by our circumstances. As James Allen wrote in *As a Man Thinketh*, "Circumstance does not make a man, it reveals him." This is one of the most important laws of human nature. Our circumstances are just a reflection of what is going on inside our world of thoughts, emotions and beliefs.

PRIVATE THOUGHTS DON'T STAY PRIVATE FOR LONG

What you think about most frequently will ultimately be revealed for everyone to see. In other words, your private thoughts don't stay private for long. Human beings are really "human becomings." As we begin to change, our world changes with us. As we become better our lives become better, and the prerequisite for changing circumstances is that you must first change yourself. To have it any other way is pretending to be the tail and trying to wag the dog.

We have two choices when life doesn't go our way: We can get bitter or we can get better. Regarding our past, we can become bitter and drag that bitterness through the rest of life, or we can embrace it and deal with it, and use it as the means to positively impact others. Staying on purpose requires you to change and grow into the person you were meant to be. To do that you must get in touch with your core desires. It is these high-intensity desires, often referred to as the "DNA of success," that reveal the role you are meant to fulfill. Accept the fact that you have been custom-made to serve an exclusive function in this world, even if that role and plan to fulfill it are not yet clear to you. **This is your genius, and it's up to you to find it.**

You might ask, "If this is so compelling, why isn't everyone doing it?" After working with thousands of people over the years at the 1% Club and undertaking an enormous amount of research, my former partner Tommy Newberry came up with some strong conclusions:

1. We are all born with unique gifts and have a specific purpose to fulfill.

2. This purpose for your life will align with your unique gifts, talents and a combination of other factors.

3. The activities and pursuits that you find most enjoyable and attractive are the best indicators of strong talent and giftedness.

4. When you engage in activities that demand your special talent, your brain releases chemicals that trigger within you a sense of satisfaction and significance as an incentive for you to keep it up. It's a positive reinforcement mechanism that is part of our perfect design. These talents get converted into strengths and eventually genius if we sustain the course long enough.

5. Your unique combination of talents, life experiences and personality merge together and spark a vision or dream within you. The more you engage in your strengths, the more crystallized your ultimate vision becomes.

6. With this dream imprinted on your mind, you become very intrinsically motivated, requiring less and less prodding from the outside. You become inner-directed, and self discipline becomes effortless.

7. This whole process is contrarian and countercultural. Instead of competing to max out their potential, most people compete to keep up with each other. They are in the wrong race. Philosophically they tend to desire comfort more than character. Strategically, they often find themselves in the wrong career. Tactically, they've resigned themselves to simply enjoying their evenings, weekends and vacations. That's the very definition of the rat race. My friend Pat Morley says in his book *The Man in the Mirror*, "When you're in rat race, even if you win, you're still a rat." Think about that. "When

you're in the rat race, even if you win, you're still a rat." This leads us to…

8. The dream in your heart won't come to fruition by accident.

Naturally, there is a price for all of this, one that requires you to surrender the concept of safety and comfort in exchange for the higher and more significant reward of living the life you were intended to live, and leaving your unique mark on the world. You must grant yourself a promotion and escape from your personal comfort zone if you want to become a difference-maker. We all have the tendency to get complacent and comfortable. It's like having a box around you, and as you step beyond the borders of that box, you start to get an uneasy feeling because you don't know what lies beyond that border. As I've mentioned previously, you're afraid of what people might think if you try something and fail. You're afraid of failure itself. You're afraid of succeeding. You're afraid of the unknown, so you never wander beyond the borders of that self-contained box. I have spent most of my life trying to get myself out of that box, and, having learned how, it is now my purpose and passion to help other people and organizations get themselves out of that box.

ABANDON ALL THOUGHT OF RETREAT

All along the path you will face resistance—institutional resistance, cultural resistance, relationship resistance, financial resistance, mental resistance. Often we are our own worst enemy because of the "mind monsters" that inhabit our brain. This is simply part of the dream game. You must press on against the forces of conformity. You must take action that is committed to your ultimate vision, and you must do this *before* you have the money, *before* you have the confidence and even *before* you have the blessing of those closest to you.

The first step is unconditional resolve. You must draw a line in the sand. Then the plan will come, the resources will emerge, and—with all thought of retreat cast aside—you become an unstoppable force. It reminds me of the historical account of De Soto's landing on the shore of what is now Florida.

When the Spanish conqueror Hernando De Soto reached the New World five centuries ago, he ordered his troops inland. They marched along as ordered until they came to a rise. Looking back, they saw the smoke and flames of burning ships—the ships they'd arrived on. Now they knew they had no alternative. They could not go back. The only decision they could make was to move forward, do battle, and defeat the enemy and win the cause.

What ships do you need to burn so that you don't have an excuse to go backwards?

THE INTERSECTION OF GENIUS

Your area of genius is the intersection where what you enjoy doing most intersects with what you do best. This is the specific area where you're capable of making the greatest difference or contribution in the world. Excellence is achievable once you find your genius. You find your genius by first asking yourself what you'd do all day long if money were not a factor. Only when you really love what you do will you have what it takes on the inside to generate tremendous results on the outside.

A genius is someone who believes and takes action on the ideas and dreams inside them. We all have dreams and ideas. The only difference between dreams that come to life and dreams that don't are the actions or inactions of the dreamer. I can't tell you how many people approach me with ideas but are afraid to take the first step. I always ask them this question: "Are you willing to mortgage your house and everything you have and invest it in this idea?"

Most often the response is, "No, that's why I came to you."

My response is always, "If you're not willing to invest in it, why should I be willing to invest in it?"

The point is, most people aren't really committed to their ideas. Rather, they're committed to the *idea* of the idea, but are unwilling to follow through and sacrifice and take the steps to make it happen. Successful people follow their dreams by getting them out of their head and down on paper so they can take action on a daily basis. They don't always succeed, but they learn, they grow and have information for next time. What do you secretly want to do with your life? Can you exercise the courage to honestly identify where you have been uniquely blessed, where you have special talents and abilities? If you don't know, pray about it, ask your spouse or ask your friends. But whatever you do, seek it out.

I believe every person has the ability to become outstanding at in at least one pursuit if they are strategically selective and they throw their whole heart into it. Excellence and the abundant opportunities that come with it can only be achieved if you do what you love and love what you do, focusing on your unique strengths to the exclusion of all else.

If you're not passionate and excited about what you do, how can you expect anyone else to be?

The concept of genius is closely aligned with two major principles of peak personal performance: **The Strength Principle**, which states that by focusing on your strengths you ultimately render your weaknesses irrelevant, and the **80/20 Principle**, which states that 80 percent of your results come from only 20 percent of your input. Over the course of my career, I have seen it time and time again. In business, 20 percent of your clients, 20 percent of your customers, 20 percent of your actions, will produce 80 percent of your results. In relationships, it's the same way: 20 percent of your input creates 80 percent of what comes out the other side.

What exactly is your genius? Your genius is a set of related activities that, collectively, produce superior results in the marketplace, whether you're an athlete, a pastor, a business leader, an entrepreneur, in law enforcement or a teacher. Everyone has a marketplace, a group of people they are charged with serving in one way or another. When you operate in your genius, you produce outstanding results. Best of all, these outcomes are generated with an investment of time and effort that is disproportionately small—as long as it's properly calculated.

Your genius is where you are most fully leveraged. This is where you can work less and earn more. This is where you can do less but become much more. This is where you can significantly increase the dollar value of each hour of your time. This is where you're capable of making the greatest difference or contribution in the world and create the most influence on others.

"Courage is rightly the foremost of virtues for upon it all others depend."

WINSTON CHURCHILL

Almost everyone has experienced brief glimpses of genius, yet only a small percentage have capitalized on their potential and transformed it into their daily operating system. When most people look back on their lives, they don't regret the things they did as much as the things they didn't do. How many times have you wanted to do something that you knew would make you and the people around you better off, but you hesitated out of fear? It takes courage to push beyond our fears.

HOW TO IDENTIFY YOUR GENIUS

How can you best acknowledge and understand what you were uniquely wired to do? These six clues will help you identify your genius.

1. Be passionate: Your area of genius is characterized by enthusiasm, intent, interest and pure fun. This passion will be difficult to turn off even when you're away from work. You'll have boundless energy. Working in your area of genius will energize you physically, mentally and emotionally, and when you do experience fatigue it is accompanied by a powerful sense of satisfaction. On the flipside, non-genius activity drains your energy.

Norman Vincent Peale shared the story about a trapeze instructor who was teaching a group of people. After getting some basic instruction on the ground, they had to climb way up the pole and stand on a little platform waiting to launch out and jump for the trapeze. One particular young man froze like a deer in headlights. The instructor shouted out to the young man, "Throw your heart over the bar and the rest of your body will follow." Your heart is your emotional center, the control panel for the rest of your body. Whatever that bar is in your life, being passionate about it is part of the process of understanding your genius.

When we started Trillium Health Products, I commuted between Atlanta and Seattle. On plane rides I would ask people about what they were eating, and they'd ask me what I did for a living. My response was, "Well, I have a company and our mission is to educate people about good health and nutrition and provide them with products to live a healthy and nutritional lifestyle." Inevitably, they'd start pushing their airline food away because I was so passionate about talking to people about what I did. Whether flying to or from Seattle, the person sitting next to me would usually wind up purchasing a juicer after witnessing my passion.

How often do you talk about what you do for a living? When you're out socially, when you're around other people, when you're having lunch, when you're at the ballpark? I'm not talking about being overbearing and always trying to sell somebody, but the first time you meet people, the first question they ask is: "What do you do for a living?" Do you respond with passionate enthusiasm or do you just say, "I'm a clerk."

Lyndon Johnson was on a tour of NASA's Mission Control in Houston when he came across a particularly energetic and enthusiastic janitor. Johnson said, "Young man, I just can't get over it. I never met a janitor who was as energetic and as passionate as you are." The young man replied, "Mr. President, I'm not just a janitor. I'm part of a team of people that put a man on the moon!"

How do you think about what you do? Are you just a janitor? Or are you part of a team of people that put a man on the moon? The way you think about what you do makes all the difference about the passion and energy you exude to other people and if you aren't passionate about what you do, how can you expect anyone else to be?

2. Never stop learning: In your area of genius, you'll notice that learning new information takes little time and comes quite easily. New concepts are easily visualized and quickly integrated into your existing knowledge base. Just as important, the learning process is fun. Never-ending improvement comes naturally. Your area of genius is characterized by a vivid, clear and almost perfect memory. Facts, figures, dates, names, conversations and key points related to your genius activities are effortlessly recalled when needed.

I'm a voracious reader on the subject of health and fitness. I love to read articles and books that talk about the latest breakthroughs. I make it a point to stay up on it, not just so I can share it with everybody else, but so I know for myself and I can take advantage of cutting-edge information. **You have to be a continuous learner in order to become a continuous earner.** The more you learn and the more you can apply your new information to helping other people, the more you're going to be compensated.

3. Maintain unstoppable momentum: When you're operating in your genius, you'll be totally immersed in what you're doing and lose yourself in the moment. You'll lose track of time. World-class athletes sometimes refer to this as being "in the zone." Researchers have also called this phenomenon "flow." It's when you're totally absorbed in the present moment and able to shut out everything else.

When do you feel "in the zone?" For me, it's when I'm in front of groups of people (or for that matter just one person) sharing what I've learned to help get them unstuck. I get so passionate that it creates unstoppable momentum toward success.

4. Follow your gut: In your genius, you'll naturally tap into your intuition and be inclined to go for it. Let me add: You'll be right most of the time. You will experience a strong, instinctual knowledge that helps you make quick, positive decisions that move you towards your goal. I remember one specific decision I made when we were involved in a lawsuit with another company over a trademark violation. We had already spent hundreds of thousands of dollars on this lawsuit, and almost 50 percent of my time was focused on this issue, rather than being creative and helping my business grow. I was sitting with our attorneys one day and I asked, "Well, what does the next four or five months look like?"

"We're going to have to spend several hundred thousand more dollars and there are going to be 40 to 50 depositions," said one.

"And what is the outcome going to be? We're going to win this case?" I asked.

Even though we were correct legally, morally and ethically, the lawyers said we had only a 70 percent chance of winning the case. In other words, we were totally in the right and there was a 30 percent chance that we were going to lose. My instincts said, "This is not right. I've got to stop spending the money and wasting my time." I announced to the room that I was going to phone the CEO of the other company.

"You can't do that!" they all said at once.

I disregarded their advice and went with my instincts. I called the CEO on the other side and said, "I'm spending hundreds of thousands of dollars, and expending a massive amount of time and effort and energy, and you must be doing the same. If you'll agree to a cease-and-desist order, I will drop the lawsuit." In five minutes, we had a deal. Because I was working in my genius, my instincts were correct and I regained a vast amount of time and money to use for better purposes. Your instincts will work for you when you're working in your zone and in your genius.

5. Say goodbye to burnout: By operating in your genius, you will insulate yourself from burning out since you'll be working at what you love to do. You will get more done in less time and be happier, healthier and much more balanced.

Burnout is the mental, emotional and physical consequence of overwork in an area of weakness, or non-genius. In other words when you identify your strength, the more you work in it, the more energy, health and vitality you have. When you work in your non-genius areas, it sucks the energy out of you. Burnout is the breaking-point result of accumulated resistance to non-genius activity. If you're not working in your genius and you yearn to be working in another area, take this as a sign that you have yet to discover your genius.

Here's an incredible statistic—Gallup surveyed more than two million people at companies around the world and asked them this question: "Do you get to use your greatest strength every day at work?" Amazingly, 8 out of 10—80 percent!—said they do not get to use their greatest strength every day at work. That means that 80 percent of us are yearning to work in our genius, but the environment we work in doesn't allow it. Companies are losing billions of dollars collectively because people aren't working at what they do best.

I realize that at times we all need to do certain things. When you have a boss and you're working for a company, it is very difficult to launch out on your own and do your own thing. But the more you can gravitate towards understanding what you do best, the more positive contributions you'll make to the company. If you run your own business, it will help create more revenue and more downtime for you to spend with your family.

6. Wing it: For a good portion of my life, I would do little prep before I got up and spoke to people. I would just get up and wing it because I really didn't know any better, and I was amazed that I received great feedback. If there's something in your life you do well and get great results from without much preparation, pay attention to that. It might be a sign that you are working in your genius.

The above are all clues to discovering your genius. What follows are the **roadblocks to finding your genius.** When you notice these roadblocks, go around them or over them or through them. You owe it to your team and to yourself.

The foreign-concept roadblock: Most people are unaware of the concept of genius and thus are uncomfortable associating themselves with it. It's simply inconsistent with their self-concept. To most of the world, work is something done for the sole purpose of paying bills, and enjoying evenings, weekends and, ultimately, retirement. In that same Gallup poll mentioned above, 86 percent of the people reported that they would rather be in another line of work. In one business I owned, I asked a person during an interview, "Why did you leave your other company?"

"I didn't enjoy working there," he replied.

"How long did you work there?" I asked.

"Seven years."

"How could you spend seven years working someplace where you didn't enjoy what you were doing?" I asked. He had no answer for this.

Don't get me wrong. I know we all need to make a living, I know we need to put food on the table. I know we need to take care of our families. But the more you work towards your genius, the more you can work towards your passion, the more you can plug into what you were put on this earth to do, the more productive your results will be, and the more influence and the more impact you're going to have on others. Your success blesses other people, and the more you can apply yourself and understand how to do this, the bigger and better your contributions will be.

They don't teach you these things in school. When one of my children was a junior in high school, she scored 780 out of 800 on the math portion of the S.A.T.'s, and 150 points lower in English. The amazing thing is that the school counselor *didn't* say, "Wow, you're a math genius, you should focus on that. There are so many opportunities out there that will use that that gift." Instead, the counselor said, "You're great at math, but you need to work on your English and bring that up."

That makes no sense to me whatsoever. In the real world, you get paid for your strengths, not your weaknesses. Why shouldn't we focus on our strengths? I understand that in high school you need to be exposed to a lot of things, but by the time you're a junior, you have a pretty good idea of where you excel and where you don't. For the most part, our educational systems—and our corporate systems—are not structured to help people understand what their strengths are and how to leverage those strengths.

The obstacle of inertia: You remember the statement, "A body at rest tends to stay at rest unless acted upon by an outside force?" That's the grade-school definition of inertia. Most people have no outside force to get them moving, and the longer they've been operating in a stagnant system, the greater the force needed to move them. A little taste of success, mixed with some comfort and security, often suppresses the desire for phenomenal success. In other words, success tends to breed complacency.

I saw it in my own company when we grew it from zero to $100 million in a short period of time. Once we had some success, we lost the "bootstrap mentality" that got us to that point. In short, we stopped doing the things that created our success and started resting on the money in the bank. It's human nature to get comfortable and forget what got us there, but I've learned that's a weak spot in human nature. You always need to keep pushing the envelope. You're either growing, and moving forward, or you're moving backwards. There is no middle ground.

Bureaucracy and red tape: A bureaucratic organization seldom provides employees with the opportunity to achieve full leverage and support in their area of genius. Strangely enough, bureaucracies tend to promote away from unique strength and genius, not towards it. This is common with sales superstars who get promoted to sales manager only to under-perform or burn out.

"The Peter Principle," where employees get promoted one time too many, illustrates this bureaucratic barrier. At Trillium Health Products, as I mentioned before, we grew from two to 225 people. I found that every time we doubled in size, the person who had been the perfect manager in a given position quickly became obsolete, because they could not handle fast-track growth. It's not a reflection on that person. The company simply outgrew their experience. I found we needed to hire people for where we were going, not where we'd been or where we were.

The Lone Ranger mentality: This approach works for a while and then you and your horse hit a wall. I've seen many a startup superstar who wouldn't give up certain parts of their business to others, even if it would improve production. Some don't want to share the credit or split the pie into another piece, even if it means the pie would be much bigger. This is called the "scarcity mentality," and it's the opposite of huge thinking.

I know what I know, but more importantly, I know what *I don't know*. Most of my success has come from surrounding myself with people who were much smarter than me. Someone once said, it would be amazing what we could accomplish if we didn't care who got credit for doing it. That person was right. If you are part of a team that's working together with a consistent vision and mission, it will improve the productivity of everybody when you empower them to do what they need to do. When you sustain them, encourage them, compliment them, praise them and then constantly communicate your vision, the environment will be such that goals have a much higher chance of being realized.

The roadblock of mediocre hiring: This one's quite obvious—you get what you pay for. Some of the biggest breakthroughs for our clients occur when they hire an extremely able assistant who can take care of their non-genius workload. They become much more productive. With an average support staff, you'll never acquire the confidence to unload the activities that are holding you back the most. With good support staff, your output won't just be increased, it will be multiplied. You can double or even triple your results over time.

When I was a partner in the 1% Club, the people who were engaged in and practiced our coaching and accountability techniques doubled or tripled their income in 12 to 18 months. This is not only possible, it's probable. And if you diligently apply these principles to your entire life, you will see results. It won't happen passively or conservatively, you must be willing to break convention. You must be revolutionary or maybe even somewhat eccentric. When you've risen to the next peak of super-effectiveness, you'll find it hard to believe you used to operate in any other way.

When I was trying to find my genius, I sent a letter to the people around me—people that I worked with, some family members, some friends, and people who had interacted with me on business dealings. I asked them two questions: "In your observation, what are my greatest strengths?" and "What do you feel I am most passionate about?"

You can send the same letter, and it will either validate what you already know or help you identify things that you weren't aware of. When we are acting in our genius, it comes so naturally, we're often not aware of it. The other part of this? You realize that those genius things you've been giving away for free can earn you compensation.

If you still think you need more help in determining your genius after using the clues I've given you, and sending letters to those people around you and receiving feedback, there are a variety of places you can find tests and assessments that will help you uncover your genius. One of my favorites is located at www.thediscpersonalitytest.com, and is a series of tests from Kolbe (www.Kolbe.com) that I've found very helpful. Another assessment I've used is called the StrengthsFinder

Test (www.strengthsfinder.com). Finally, I recommend the book *Now, Discover Your Strengths*, by Marcus Buckingham and Donald O. Clifton, Ph.D. It offers several resources to find assessments.

CHAPTER 5:

WHEN THE WILL TO WIN MEETS THE WILL TO PREPARE

"I'm not afraid to die on a treadmill. I will not be outworked.
You may be more talented than me. You might be smarter than
me. And you may be better looking than me. But if we get on
a treadmill together you are going to get off first or I'm going to
die. It's really that simple. I'm not going to be outworked."

WILL SMITH

I remember when I was a senior at Valhalla High School in New York. I was part of the two mile relay team. We were the last event of the meet against our cross-town rivals. If we won, we'd win the meet. I usually ran in the number two spot, but our coach moved me to the anchor position (the key number four spot) because he knew we needed to do something different to get a better time. My previous best time in the half mile event was 2:21 (2 minutes and 21 seconds). It was a close race and I had a 10-foot advantage over our rival as I was handed the baton. I knew I couldn't let my team and my coach down. I ran like someone was trying to kill me. I would not let the other racer pass me and I crossed the finish line just ahead of him, in a time of

2:03, and as I crossed the line, I fell down from exhaustion. *I left it all on the course.*

YOU CAN FACE THE PAIN OF DISCIPLINE NOW OR THE PAIN OF REGRET LATER

We all have the will to win. But the will to win without the will to prepare to win is nothing. The only place in which "success" comes before "work" is in the dictionary. There is no easy, pain-proof route to success.

What we continually forget is that it takes sacrifice and discipline to build and maintain anything that is worthwhile in life. Whether it's your marriage, your family, your health or your business, we get what we put in and we reap what we sow. How you perform on "game day," whether that's a football game or your presentation to a new client—is determined by what you do to prepare seven days, seven weeks, seven months and even seven years in advance.

Whether you're a pro athlete, a heart surgeon, or a retail salesperson, this formula holds true. You can make it to a certain level on *talent* alone. You can make it to a certain level on *discipline* alone. You can make it to a certain level on *passion* alone. But when you have all three working together, you are an unstoppable force.

Discipline + talent + passion = unstoppable force

There are a lot of very talented people who are not performing to their full potential because they avoid rigorous preparation. Discipline— and the will to prepare—is the X factor that will take whatever talent and passion you have to the next level and beyond.

Here are six steps to becoming more disciplined and putting the X-Factor to work in your life.

1. Be a true student of your craft or profession

To continue earning more, you have to keep learning more. What can you do to learn more about your profession? The more you can learn, the more you can contribute to it. What can you read? What seminars can you attend? In general, the more you learn about your profession, the more you'll be compensated.

2. Give more value than you're paid for

I can't overemphasize this. When you "go the extra mile," you won't find many other competitors on the road. Give your customers, your employees, your colleagues and your family more than they expect. When you bring more value to the table than expected, people respond positively. And that goes for everyone, in all areas of life.

For example, when I speak to a group, I go the extra mile by calling some members in the group ahead of time and asking, "What do you really hope to get out of the seminar?" I'll ask what their greatest challenges are at the current time. I'll ask how the time that I'll be with them would be most profitable to them.

The benefits of this are clear: I give a targeted presentation that's tailored directly to the group I'm addressing that day, and I know that people won't be leaving the seminar disappointed.

The downside? I don't have the luxury of doing canned presentations.

"In 17 years, you're the only speaker who ever called ahead of time and asked these questions, and I really appreciate it," one company representative said to me. I received invitations to do six more talks based on his recommendations.

What can you do to "go the extra mile" in your business? Give that question some serious thought. In your job, what's one thing you can do to go the extra mile internally, for the people you're working with, and what's one thing you can do externally, for your customers or the industry?

What is one thing you can do to go the extra mile in your relationship, or with your family, or your community?

Take a moment to think about this and write these down.

3. Don't hope to succeed. *Expect* to succeed

The more you prepare, the more you can expect to achieve the outcome or result that you want. The less you prepare, the more you will hope to achieve the outcome or result that you want.

Given the preparation I put into each talk I give, I don't hope to connect with the audience and deliver exactly what they're looking for. I *expect* to connect with the audience and to give them the specific information, motivation, and other tangibles that they came to the seminar expecting to receive. I've already put in the effort on the front end to ensure that.

HOPE IS NOT A STRATEGY FOR SUCCESS

During the 1990s and early 2000s, when the Atlanta Braves won 14 straight National League East division titles, someone asked Chipper Jones, one of their All-Star players, "Why are the Braves so successful?"

He replied, "When we step on the field we expect to win. The other teams hope they'll win."

When you expect to win, your confidence level will grow. As you prepare to win, your expectations to achieve the outcomes you want to achieve will grow.

You need to expect to succeed. But that is not enough. You must prepare in advance for that to happen.

When you call on a sales prospect, do you hope to get the sale or do you expect to get the sale? If your marriage is currently rocky, do you hope to one day have a better marriage, or do you expect to have a better marriage? How you respond to these questions can reveal a great deal about why you have—or have not—achieved the goals you want to achieve. In business, and in life, hopes often go unanswered.

You don't get what you want in life. You get what you expect.

When we first started Trillium Health Products and began marketing the *Juiceman Juicer*, we created a plan to give free seminars about health and nutrition. During these seminars, we demonstrated our juicer—which was conveniently for sale at the back of the room during the seminar. Over a year and a half, we gave free seminars to 650,000 people. And those people told us, face-to-face, everything that they liked and didn't like about our product.

My brother Rick and I sat in the back of the room and took extremely detailed notes during these seminars. When "The Juice Man" was talking, there would be spontaneous moments when a person (or a group of people) would get up and go to the back of the room to purchase our Juicer. When that happened, we would write down exactly what he said during those moments before they got up to buy the Juicer.

We continually refined and tweaked the seminar until we knew—with great reliability—that 22.6 percent of the people who attended the free seminar would buy a Juicer.

Now, let's fast forward 12 months. We were putting together a direct marketing TV program, aka an infomercial. I took all of the information that we had learned over a year and a half of the seminars and applied it to a direct marketing program.

Given my research and my notes, I knew the words we needed to say. I knew the concepts and specific selling points that made people get up and purchase our product. When we put it on TV in an infomercial, we didn't hope it would work; we expected it to work. We had done our homework. And the infomercial was just as effective as the seminars.

We knew it would be.

Had we not gone through all of that preparation with the free seminars, and just put together a TV marketing plan without knowing how people would respond to the selling points, we would have lost a lot of time, effort, and money.

Now, don't get me wrong. Just because you prepare meticulously in advance and you do everything you're supposed to do doesn't mean you can control the outcome with utter certainty. But when you prepare in advance, and put great effort into that preparation, you are drastically increasing the odds of achieving the outcome you seek.

4. Become an expert

In the hours you'll spend preparing for success, you can reap an extremely worthwhile and unexpected reward that may change the course of your life.

You become an expert in a specific field or topic.

How much time? In his book *Outliers*, author Malcolm Gladwell wrote that it takes 10,000 hours of focused practice at a fairly high level to become an expert at whatever profession you choose to pursue. This typically takes a minimum of 10 years.

This makes sense, whether you're looking at doctors or lawyers, or professional football or basketball players. Many start working on their craft early, whether through reading or hobbies, or organized team sports. Especially for athletes, their practice usually intensifies greatly through the four years of high school and four additional years in college. If they join the pro ranks right out of college, most need two more years of solid practice before they start performing well.

Quarterback Peyton Manning of the Indianapolis Colts is a prime example. He had losing seasons his first two years as a pro and didn't play particularly well, but in the years that followed he set the standard for quarterback play in the NFL. That's certainly 10-plus years of dedicated practice. It's not difficult to see how someone could compile 10,000 hours of active experience if they live, eat and breathe their sport or profession during that decade.

Again, it's more than just putting in time. If you've been driving an automobile for 30 years, you're probably no more proficient at it now than you were 15 years ago—even though you've put in thousands of hours of "practice time." Those 10,000 hours need to be spent performing at a challenging level that forces you to learn and grow—and an important part of that process in many fields is spending time around other people who are performing at an extremely high level.

5. Eat the frog first

Preparation work isn't glamorous work. It's often grunt work. It's poring over data and information, taking notes and performing tasks that seldom bring the word "fun" to mind. But since it's so critical to your ultimate success, and it can't be done half-heartedly, I'll share a tactic I use to make it easier.

It's a concept called "eat the frog first," and it was developed by self-help author Brian Tracy. It's simple, but ruthless: Do the absolute worst task first.

The frog represents the important thing that you hate to do the most, but will have the greatest impact towards reaching your goal. And you have to eat it. First.

It's pretty disgusting to think about eating a frog, and I'm not sure that putting it in a juicer would make it much better. Here's why you're going through this horrible thought exercise: If you eat the frog first, *anything* else you eat afterwards will taste pretty doggone good.

The frog is that task that you don't want to tackle, but if you did, it would have the greatest impact on creating the results you're trying to accomplish.

One of my frogs is writing. I hate to write. It is very difficult for me to sit down and write. I have difficulty focusing for long periods of time, so writing is incredibly tedious. Lately, this has been a problem that I just can't avoid. In creating a book, writing is pretty important, isn't it? What typically happens with me is that I will look for *anything* else I can possibly do besides writing. And there are usually hundreds of options. But ultimately, when I procrastinate and I don't do the writing I need to do, it makes me feel less productive because I know I didn't do the most important thing I need to do.

I'm sure you have the same feeling when you don't do the thing you know you really need to do. It sets off a chain of events that mentally take you down a very gloomy path. When you procrastinate, you're sabotaging yourself and you know it, so harboring negative feelings and chastising yourself is both logical and expected.

On the other hand, when I do the writing first thing in the morning and get it out of the way—I eat the frog first, so to speak—I feel on top of the world and ready to take on more tasks.

So I do it first. I eat the frog first. And then the rest of the chores that must get done seem much easier in comparison. Plus, I feel energized, elated and productive. Instead of procrastinating, I got the *difficult, but most important thing* done first!

What is the frog in your life? What is the dreaded task you avoid at almost any cost—but know that if you did it, you would be much better off?

Eat that frog right now.

BEATING PROCRASTINATION

Eating the frog often means overcoming procrastination. You must win the battle against procrastination to rise above the average. I struggled with this for a long time. Peak performance and procrastination simply do not go together.

Procrastination is the delaying of higher priority tasks in favor of lower priority tasks. It's responsible for more frustration, stress and underachievement than any other single factor. Procrastination causes emotional anguish, devastates personal relationships, wrecks any attempt at effectiveness and promotes physical and mental exhaustion.

Procrastination is all about excuses, and we all know that the excuses you have today are the excuses you will have tomorrow. **Remember, tomorrow changes today.** You have to break the procrastination habit today in order to have a better, brighter tomorrow.

So how can you defeat procrastination and start creating results? The hardest part of getting started is simply getting started. You need to develop a sense of urgency. Once you've begun, you've overcome the toughest hurdle. You don't always have to start at the beginning. If the first step seems hard or too large, start with another part of the project. Or set a mini goal such as working at something for 15 minutes, whether it's reading, exercising or a work project. Often—after 15 minutes, you'll want to continue. You may even complete the entire task.

6. Find a mentor or a coach. I can't overemphasize how important it is to learn directly from somebody who has achieved success in the area that you're pursuing. The best athletes at the top of their game, in every single sport, have a coach or a mentor to help them play what we call their "A" game.

A lot of professional athletes can make it to the top level of competition on talent alone. They could cut it in the pros and be an average player.

FROM FROGS TO ELEPHANTS

Question: How do you eat an elephant?

Answer: One small piece at a time. And that's how you tackle any large project without giving in to procrastination. You forget about the overwhelming whole and start doing it one small piece at a time.

But when they take the discipline of preparing every day with their passion, and they get a coach or a mentor to continually help them play their position better, it can take them to the elite level.

If you want to become an expert in your industry or field, you need to find a mentor. Find a person who has already achieved success in the field and, if you don't have a personal connection with them, ask them for an hour of their time.

And pay them if necessary.

I have done this many times. I've paid people their hourly rate to sit down and pick their brains. I have paid people $1,000 to sit down with them for 90 minutes of their time. You might think that's crazy, but what if I tell you that those 90 minutes gave me an idea that generated $50,000 in revenue? Would that sound crazy? This actually happened to me. I consulted with a seasoned expert when I was in the middle of negotiating a contract with a client, and the advice he gave me netted an additional $50,000 of income in the first 60 days of the deal. People have paid me thousands of dollars for my advice, and some of them have made millions from it.

I've paid mentors for their advice, but there have been many other people who gave me free advice, or took the time to coach me and mentor me without asking for payment. These relationships and the wisdom they've imparted have been the basis for some of my most satisfying successes in several areas of my life.

For example, my wife and I knew an older couple that mentored us on how to be a better husband and a better wife. We looked to them for this purpose because they expressed the same values and stood for the same principles that we did. We said to them, "Look, 25 years from now, we'd love to have a relationship like you have. What do we need to do?" They talked to us at length and they gave us the benefit of their wisdom.

I can't tell you how many times in business I have reached out to people for advice.

And it's often unbelievable how eager people are to share their wisdom with you, to give you the benefit of their experience. Just make certain that wisdom is truly all you're seeking. If your motives are suspect, or if you want to get something other than advice from an expert or a potential mentor, you're using that person and asking to be burned.

I remember a young man who called me and said he really admired my accomplishments, and asked if I would be willing to have a cup of coffee with him. I knew this young man's parents, though I didn't know him very well, so I agreed to spend an hour with him.

When I showed up for this meeting, he brought his boss with him. He didn't tell me he was bringing anyone with him, which was discourteous and unprofessional. To make matters worse, his boss had one motive: To persuade me to buy the product he was selling. I sat at that table for an excruciating 30 minutes. Then I said, "I'm sorry, I'm going to have to cut this meeting short. Thank you and have a good day."

I promptly telephoned this young man. "I'm really disappointed," I said to him. "I was prepared to give you an hour of my time and to give you some wisdom that I have learned over the last 30 years. But instead, I hope you'll learn a valuable lesson from the mistake you made today." In a nutshell, I told him to always let people know what your agenda is for requesting a meeting, and to always inform them that other people will be attending (or ask their permission before inviting other people). I told him it would be a long time before I would agree to meet with him again.

That might sound pretty harsh. But I believe that it was the best thing I could have done for that young man in the situation, to help him learn. You must have the right motives when you ask someone to give you their advice. You have to care about the other person. If you don't, you've broken a social contract that has helped generations of highly motivated, ethical people achieve their dreams. When you find someone who will graciously coach or mentor you—even if you're paying them—always remember to ask, "How can I help you in return?"

USE A PEN, NOT A KEYBOARD

When you meet with somebody and they give you your time, write them a handwritten note. Especially these days, a handwritten note of appreciation means so much more than an email. People aren't used to getting handwritten notes any more, so sending a handwritten note will really make you stand out.

Being a mentor can be extremely rewarding—in a lot of ways. The more people you help, the more chances there are for help to come your way when you need it. The natural law of giving is that when you help someone, it just seems to come back to you in ways that you could never imagine.

But again, when it comes to mentoring, you must give to give, with no expectation that you're going to get something in return. If you give to get, it's typically very obvious to the other party. And it's often self-sabotaging.

FINDING POTENTIAL MENTORS

The following exercise will help you identify the people whom you can tap for advice and wisdom, in order to help you achieve the goals you've set. Contact potential mentors for those areas of focus that are relevant to you and your goals. The exercises are excerpted from a workbook I developed with Tommy Newbury for a CD series entitled *Success Is Not an Accident, Secrets of the Top 1%*, available from www.VitalVisionsInc.com.

1. Pick an area of focus:

   - Sales
   - Marketing
   - Health
   - Marriage
   - Spiritual Growth
   - Parenting

2. Identify potential candidates who demonstrate the following characteristics:

   - High integrity
   - Exceptionally experienced
   - Proven track record
   - Leader in their field

Name your candidates below:

_____

_____

_____

_____

3. Develop your plan:

   ASK: "I would really value a little bit of your time each month to mentor me. This would just mean a 10-15 minute phone call each month where I could ask you a few questions. Would you be open to that?"

   Create your own strategy and structure for this relationship.

   YES: schedule the first appointment.

   NO: ask for a referral, or if they might reconsider at another time. Move on to the next person on the list as necessary.

This chapter about preparing to succeed is worth putting a bookmark in. There is no shortcut to success; it takes time, preparation, and experience. There is no easy path or magic bullet to take you there. You must put in the time and effort to get the results you want, on the way to creating the success you've envisioned for yourself.

You need to expect to accomplish these goals. And in order to expect them, you have to increase your levels of *preparation* and *discipline*. The more disciplined you become about preparing, the more confidence you're going to build, and the better you're going to perform at any pursuit—whether it's getting a big sale, getting a big date, or accomplishing any other goal.

Again, you'll be tapping into the equation that allows you to truly flourish: *talent* plus *passion* plus *discipline* equals an *unbeatable force* in almost any realm, from golf to football, banking to medicine, art to politics.

The final ingredient is experience; having a mentor or a coach can be an incredible help.

I hope, no, I EXPECT you'll use the strategies in this chapter to bring it all together.

CHAPTER 6:

GET RID OF THE JUNK!

"Stop acting as if life is a rehearsal. Live this day as if it were your last. The past is over and gone. The future is not guaranteed."

WAYNE DYER

In 1845, a lavishly equipped two-ship expedition led by Sir John Franklin sailed from England to the Canadian Arctic to chart the last unknown parts of the Northwest Passage. The crew loaded their sailing ships with non-essential cargo: A 1,200-volume library, fine china, crystal goblets and sterling silver tableware. Amazingly, each ship carried just a twelve-day supply of coal for its auxiliary steam engines.

Confidence was high, given that there was less than 300 miles of unexplored Arctic mainland coast by then.

When the ships failed to return after two years, relief expeditions and search parties explored the Canadian Arctic—which resulted in a thorough charting of the region, along with a possible passage. Many artifacts from the expedition were found over the next century and a half, including notes revealing what had happened to the ships and the crew.

They had become trapped in ice about halfway through the passage, near King William's Island, unable to break free. After several months in the trapped ship, Lord Franklin died and the men decided to trek to safety in small groups, but none survived. One story is especially heartbreaking: Two officers pulled a large sled more than 60 miles across the treacherous terrain. When rescuers found their bodies they discovered that the sled was filled with table silver.

Those two officers contributed to their own demise by dragging behind them what they didn't need. But don't we all sometimes do the same thing? Don't we drag junk through life that we don't need? I don't mean crates of silverware. I mean negative thoughts and memories that hinder us, bad habits that drag us down, grudges we won't let go of, and false beliefs about ourselves and others.

EVERYONE HAS SOMETHING FROM THEIR PAST THAT THEY ARE TRYING TO OVERCOME

The more I talk with people, and take time to really hear their stories, the more I realize we all have junk that we drag through life. And if you take the time—and I mean *really* take the time to talk with people, getting below the surface talk and listening carefully—you will find that everyone has something from their past that they are trying to overcome.

I'm no exception. I've already shared with you the story of my dad's death, and the huge void it left in my life. That was my first experience, at age 13, with life-changing grief. I would soon face another tragedy, one that would prove even more devastating.

Two years after my dad passed away, my four-year-old brother, Johnny, drowned in a lake on our property in New York. While I was watching TV, one of our neighbors came running in and said, "Johnny fell in the lake and David can't find him." David was my other brother.

I ran down to the lake. I remember David standing on the raft, panicked, and just screaming, "I can't find Johnny!" I took off my shirt and pants and dove into the lake. I swam frantically, trying to find my brother. But I couldn't. Neither could the rest of my family.

Within hours, several hundred people were lined up around the fence outside our lake. There were ambulances, fire trucks, and police cars. Out on the water was a rescue boat with those hooks they throw overboard when they want to find a body.

I remember standing there, after three hours, as they finally found my little brother.

I was 15. I was just starting to recover from the loss of my dad. I didn't know how to deal with the grief of this loss, and, in time, it became more heavy baggage that I carried through life.

Several years later, we would lose my brother David, too.

David was five years behind me in school. He was a fine athlete and a leader as well, the captain of his West Point baseball team. In May of 1983, my family was planning a big reunion up at West Point to celebrate his graduation. On a Sunday morning two weeks before David's commencement, someone from the college phoned our home. There had been an auto accident the night before, after a baseball game. My brother was a passenger in a car that was part of the accident. He had been killed instantly. Still today, I can't hold back tears when I recall that awful loss. A huge void still wells up in me.

My brother's funeral was held at West Point. Instead of gathering there for a family reunion and graduation festivities, we stood together in shock and grief. The night before David's funeral, on Friday evening, the cadets gathered in what they call The Quad for a moment of silence at midnight. And they called out the full Corps of Cadets. And after that moment of silence, they played taps. It was just like a scene from a movie.

If you've never been to West Point, it is in an incredible setting. I see it as vividly today as I did when I was experiencing it so many years ago. On the day of the funeral, I remember going to the banks of the Hudson River, and arriving at the cathedral where they were having his service. The band was playing "America the Beautiful" as they brought the American flag-draped casket into the chapel. Then the mourners filed in. There must have been 1,500 people in that chapel.

The family members had been asked if we wanted to give a eulogy, or just take a moment to say something about David. I didn't volunteer. My older sister said a few words. Then many West Point cadets, teachers, coaches and friends of David's spoke. Hearing their words, I realized I had feelings and thoughts I needed to share. I made my way to the front of the chapel and looked out at the crowd of people.

I told a few brief stories of the things my brother and I had done together. I mentioned the time when I was his coach in high school, and also his substitute teacher. He and a bunch of the other football players were in my seventh period class, and I fell asleep because I was up till 3 a.m. the night before. When I woke up, they were all gone!

Finally, I said, "Out of all the things I did with my brother, I never told him that I loved him. Don't wait until it's too late. Tell the people who are closest to you how much they mean to you and how much you love them because you never know how much more time you're going to have to spend with them."

I'm not sharing these stories so you will feel sorry for me. I've had difficult losses of loved ones that have shaped who I am. I share these stories to emphasize that, in some way, shape or form; we are all adult children of dysfunctional families. We all have pain and tragedy weighing on us, and we really have two choices in life: We can drag our past with us, use it as an excuse for why we can't succeed, or we can learn to live with it and use it to help other people.

It's common to try and keep the worst of this "bad stuff" locked away. The deepest, darkest secrets we carry have a huge effect, despite the silence around them. It could be the pain we feel from the loss of a loved one, or from an action or a mistake that we made in the past and still regret. We think that if anybody ever knew these secrets, they would never respect us or talk to us again. But when you bring that thing out into the open, and deal with it, it not only frees you up to become everything you were meant to be, but it also becomes a great opportunity to help others who are struggling with the same issue.

I have personally found that in my life, those secrets that I've kept, and the things that I regard as tragic mistakes or regrets—when I brought them out in the open, it freed me. It gave me the opportunity to say to someone who was hurting, "I've been where you are, and here's how I got unstuck. If I can do it, you can do it, too."

Of course, it took me time to reach that point.

THE SEX, DRUGS, ROCK-N-ROLL ERA

Most of my life, I didn't deal with the junk I had dragged around. I used it as an excuse to go through what I call the sex, drugs, rock-n-roll era of my life. I was trying to mask the pain and loss that I felt with external things. But I learned that regardless of what I did to mask the pain, I would wake up the next day to find my junk was still there.

If you're struggling with personal issues and pain, and trying to mask it, you'll learn what I learned, if you're fortunate. You can do lots of things to mask that pain, but until you bring it out in the open and learn to deal with it, you will never have peace.

I remember a benchmark moment that occurred when I was in church almost 20 years ago. Our minister, Frank Harrington, was preaching a sermon, talking about how we can best deal with the bad things that happened to us in the past. He related stories of people that had suffered tragedy upon tragedy, along with smaller-scale mishaps and failures.

Then he said, "There comes a point in your life when regardless of what has happened to you in your past, you need to take responsibility for who you are and where you are today." I was sitting there with hundreds of other people, but I felt like he was talking directly to me. I had so much stuff happen in my life and such trouble making sense of it all.

That sermon lit a spark under me. I took action to deal with the junk that was holding me back by seeking out the advice of a friend, Dr. Mark Crawford—and this friend just happened to charge me $175 an hour to listen to me. He said, "Steve, we all have demons running around the house, and the secret is to keep them locked in the basement so they don't take over the whole house."

And then he handed me a little skeleton key. And he said, "I want you to use this as a visual reminder that when those demons start to pop up in your life, you bring this out and lock them back in the basement." And I still carry that key with me as a visual reminder to keep my demons locked in the basement.

Now, this doesn't mean that you shouldn't deal with your issues. If you need to seek professional help, do it. **But you don't let those demons prevent you from living the life you were meant to live.** In other words, you need to let go of that junk that's holding you back. If you can't let it go, you must at least decide that you won't use it as an excuse or a reason why you can't do something in life.

If you adopt a victim mentality, it holds you back. When you think somebody owes you something, or that somebody has to do something for you because of the things that you experienced in your past, you're not letting yourself live the life that you were meant to live.

YOUR PAST DOES NOT EQUAL YOUR FUTURE

Let me ask you something: Do you have a greater commitment to your past, or a greater commitment to your future? Do you think your best days are behind you, or do you think your best days are still yet to come? You don't have to let the past failures and mistakes and events prevent you from having a compelling and bright future.

When you want to make the present better than the past, look at what happened in the past, learn something valuable from it, and do things differently in the present. If you take the time to talk with people—and, again, I mean to really dig below the surface—you will find that everyone has a story and pain from their past.

JUST WHAT IS "JUNK"?

My goal in this chapter is to get you to effectively deal with the junk all around you, and even within you that prevents you from being more productive and from becoming the person you were meant to be. I will show you how to simplify your life, and, in essence, how you can achieve more with less.

Webster's dictionary defines junk as "anything meaningless." That is a pretty good description. And I'm going to help you identify anything that's meaningless in your life and give you some tools to deal with it and discard it.

But let me give you my definition of junk: *Anything that adds complexity to your life without increasing your quality of life or your financial bottom line.* When I talk about junk, I'm talking about messes, stuff, lifestyle irritants, procrastination, filler, unnecessary complexity, energy leaks, disorganization, unfinished business, obligations, over commitment, busywork, incomplete tasks, low-payback activities, brain clutter, scams, stagnation, congestion and resistance.

JUNK IS A BYPRODUCT OF PRODUCTIVITY

Junk is a product of our past mistakes and past decisions, and a product of disorganization. *But junk is also the byproduct of productivity.* Let me give you an example. My wife Indy is an incredible cook. She loves to serve her homemade, three-cheese ravioli with sage and butter sauce. I'm getting hungry just thinking about it.

When she cooks, her goal is to create an excellent meal. But in the process she uses every pot and every pan in the kitchen. Flour ends up everywhere. Before she's finished, it really looks like a tornado came in through the kitchen.

Now, remember, the goal was to create an excellent meal: Three-cheese ravioli with sage and butter sauce. But in the process she created a mess, basically leaving a trail of junk. That's not a bad thing—unless you don't clean it up. Thankfully for her, that's something I love to do.

But most people don't clean up the junk that's the byproduct of their productivity. They let it pile up. Now, imagine starting to cook meal six when you haven't cleaned up any of junk left by the previous five meals. Imagine all the pots, pans, dishes, and silverware are still sitting in the kitchen. That would create congestion and confusion, and make it difficult for you to cook an excellent meal. It would make cooking more stressful, less fun, and the results and the quality would be extremely diminished.

You face exactly the same challenges and complexities in business and life in general. When we're productive, we sometimes leave a trail of clutter and junk behind us. And if we don't take the time to clean it up (or hire somebody to clean it up), it makes it more difficult for us to continue performing at that same level.

This means we are *always* going to have some level of junk—of mess and clutter—around us. It's a natural byproduct of life. Some of it is preventable, but some of it is not. You must deal with it swiftly and consistently, or—in time—the junk will consume you.

There are six specific types of junk that I want to identify.

1. Physical junk

The storage industry is one of the fastest-growing businesses in the country because we are all pack rats. We love to collect and accumulate junk, but we hate to part with it. And the average person accumulates a massive amount of junk.

An example: We recently sold a home in Atlanta we had lived in for almost 15 years. My wife and I raised four children in that house, and now that they are all grown up, it was simply too big for just the two of us. It was a rather large house, with ten bathrooms and seven bedrooms. And, of course when you have all those rooms, and all those shelves and spaces, you think you have to fill them up with stuff. You can't have a big, empty house, right?

In the process of preparing for the move, we found that the stuff we accumulated over time was absolutely overwhelming. There were boxes in the attic. Every closet was chock-full. We discovered possessions we didn't even know we had. My wife and I set a goal: We weren't going to put a single thing in storage. We agreed to sell or donate everything we didn't need.

It was a painful process and a very emotional one. We came up with guidelines and had dear friends hold us accountable to them. If we hadn't worn a piece of clothing or used an article for one year, it had to go. We accomplished our goal, but it wasn't easy.

Sorting through the sentimental items was the most difficult. We all have those things that we think we might want one day, but what we found out was that we really didn't need very much, as long as we had each other. In almost all cases, you're better off parting with those reminders of your past that you don't absolutely cherish. It's amazing how much you can simplify your life when you take the time to get organized and get the physical junk and clutter out of your environment.

When you keep a messy environment, it tends to make you less productive. You can control your physical environment by cleaning up the messes you have around you and staying more organized.

2. Financial junk

We all have too many credit cards. Many of us have too many bank accounts. Others have too many accounts payable and accounts receivable on top of it all. And the vast majority of people I meet don't have a financial plan, or they have an out-of-date financial plan. Not surprisingly, they find that more money is always going out than is coming in, and they're living beyond their means.

My wife and I were part of a pilot for a TV show called *The American Dream* (unfortunately, it never launched). We worked with a nationally acclaimed financial author and radio personality. And his stats showed that seven out of ten people live paycheck to paycheck and are in deep debt.

We also served on the board of an organization called Pro-Athletes Outreach, which is an organization that helps equip athletes to have a positive impact at home, at work and in the community. Through this organization, we've learned that a surprising number of former athletes are in financial ruin.

Consider some statistics for an NFL football player. They play professionally for an average of about three years. And within 12 to 18 months of leaving the game, 78 percent of former pro football players are bankrupt or divorced, or both.

Why? Financial clutter, a lack of planning, and just living for today and not planning for the future. How can a football player making

$3.5 million a year for three years be bankrupt in just 18 months? Well, it's pretty easy. They (or their spouse) spent $4 million a year.

Don't get hung up on the numbers. It doesn't matter if we're talking about $40,000 per year, $400,000, $4 million, or $40 million. It's never about the size of the income; it's always about lifestyle. Getting your financial life in order means living a lifestyle that's within your means. Countless books have been written about this subject. For our purposes, I'll sum it up this way: When you're carrying a severe financial burden, it's very difficult for you to perform at a high level.

3. Legal junk

There are legal vulnerabilities on a personal level and on a business level. I'm talking about not updating documents, or having an out-of-date will or not having a will at all. Do you know that 80 percent of people do not have a will?

One of the fastest-growing legal problems out there right now is identity theft, and this is a growing cause of legal junk (and financial junk, as a byproduct). When somebody steals your identity, it's *your* obligation and responsibility to undo the mess. For the average person, it can take six to twelve months to undo the damage that the criminal has caused.

Over those six to twelve months, spent untangling the mess caused by identity theft, a lot more damage is done. During that period, are you going to be at the top of your game? Are you going to be productive in the workplace? Are you going to be fully present in your relationships?

Of course not.

Legal junk can be the most time-consuming, energy-draining variety of junk, because it keeps growing out of control—and you can't take care of it by renting a dumpster and a team of professional cleaners.

As an example, we once hired a woman to write a book for our marketing company called *Juicing for Life*. We paid her an hourly rate to write the book, and we split the royalties with her. The average book sells about 5,000 copies, so nobody thought much about this arrangement. When we were doing our *Juiceman* advertising, the book took off. To date, it has sold almost three million copies. I'm gratified by that, but one of the byproducts of that extreme productivity was— guess what?—a mountain of legal junk.

The writer sued us, saying she had not been paid the appropriate amount of money and wanted to renegotiate. I suggested that we pursue arbitration rather than going to court, and she agreed. The attorneys were hostile, the proceedings were acrimonious, and the whole ordeal was draining a massive amount of productive energy from my life.

At one point during the arbitration, in arguing over how to divide the remaining cache of proceeds from the book that we had not yet agreed how to divide, things blew up. Both attorneys became frustrated, stood up, said some inappropriate words to each other, and were about to walk out of the room.

I stood and said, "Look, instead of trying to settle this by deciding which one of us gets the money, what if we take the money and split it fifty-fifty, and give it to the charitable organizations of our choice?"

Astonishingly, the writer and her party went into the other room, came back and agreed to the suggestion. A legal problem that had been consuming our lives for months disappeared in five minutes. Days later, my lawyer received a note from the Arbitrator, who was a former State Supreme Court Judge. It read, "Just a short note to thank you and Mr.

Cesari for your help in settling this case. Mr. Cesari's idea of benefiting charity through this settlement was very creative and thoughtful. Mediation of cases like this is clearly better than the risk, anxiety and expense of going to the courthouse. I enjoyed working with you and Mr. Cesari. Please extend to him my thanks for his assistance."

I could have fought for the remaining funds; they were significant. I could have demanded that the lawyers work it out. But instead, I came up with an expedient way to get rid of a huge legal mess—a colossal amount of legal junk—that was preventing me from focusing on my business and my life. It was worth it, many times over.

4. Mental junk

We only have the ability to focus on a limited number of things. When we spread ourselves too thin and lose focus of what's important, or we over commit our time or energy, we are heading for breakdown and failure.

Your brain is just like a computer. Your computer has a limited amount of RAM, or random access memory—and that's the immediate working memory that allows the computer to operate. When you open up several programs at once, you begin to overtax the computer's RAM. So your computer slows down. If you keep opening up more programs, what finally happens? The computer freezes or crashes.

Again, your brain is just like a computer: It has the RAM to focus intently on one or two activities at a time, and if you keep giving it more to focus on without getting rid of those attention-drainers, it will slow down and eventually crash.

When you have a dozen open programs in your brain, that's mental junk. We need to be able to compartmentalize the things we think about, to make sure we're staying focused on the things that are moving us toward our goals and helping us become the person we want to become. We need to shut down the programs that cause us to dwell on past mistakes or what we could or should have done.

5. Emotional junk

Emotional junk comes from failing to deal with negative feelings or emotions. It's guilt, resentment, fear, worry, anxiety. The pain of the emotions that I felt (but never dealt with) when my dad died, when my younger brother drowned and when my other brother was killed in a car accident—they caused me to carry around a great deal of emotional junk.

Over 35 years ago, while attending that aforementioned Dale Carnegie course, I bought one of the books they sell. I still carry it in my briefcase. Its cover is crinkled and torn and hardly recognizable, but the words on the inside still resonate today.

The title of the book is *How to Stop Worrying and Start Living*. In it, Carnegie listed some fundamental steps for overcoming worry and anxiety. I'll paraphrase the steps that I found most helpful.

Live in day-type compartments. Deal with what you can control and deal with it today. Don't project in the future what might or might not happen because you don't know what tomorrow holds. To face trouble, ask yourself this question: What is the worst that can possibly happen? I did that when I started Trillium Health Products. I thought, "What's the worst that can possibly happen?" *Well, I can go bankrupt; I can end up losing everything I've built; my reputation could suffer; people might not want to associate with me anymore because they'll see me as a failure.*

I sat down and looked at each of those fears, and took the next mental step: I prepared myself to accept the reality of them coming to fruition, and then did all the preparation I could to control the factors I could. Then I compiled another list of all the positive outcomes, being in business with my brother, fulfilling a lifetime dream, being my own boss, traveling to the West Coast and helping to educate others about good health and proper nutrition. It's a funny thing when you have two conflicting thoughts; the one you dwell on is usually the one that will come to pass. I chose to dwell on the later thoughts and develop a plan of action to make it happen, and it did!

So let me reiterate the message: Stay focused in the present. Learn from your past mistakes, learn something valuable from them, and then do things differently in the present. **Focus on now.** And then respond to what I call the WIN moment: What's Important Now? Stay focused on that, take action, and don't worry about what might or might not happen tomorrow. Action overcomes fear and worry.

6. Relationship junk

Who among us has not carried around some relationship junk that's affected every other aspect of our life? I've been married to my wife Indy for 30 years. I've noticed that when things are going well at home, things usually go well for me in business. And when things are disruptive at home, when I'm putting off dealing with an issue, it tends to flow over into my business. (Yes, it works both ways; business issues certainly tend to overflow into home life. But most people expect this, because they remain hyper-focused on their business lives. They're usually much more surprised to notice that having difficulty in their relationship will cause difficulty in their business.)

Compartmentalizing is key. When you're home, be at home. When you're doing business, do business. Try to keep them wholly separate. Sometimes you can't help it—there are emergencies. But for the most part, it's possible to compartmentalize these two major spheres of life and still deal with many unexpected issues that come up.

COMPARTMENTALIZE...MORE EFFECTIVELY THAN *THE TITANIC*

To repeat, compartmentalize—and keep those compartments, those boundaries, intact. *The Titanic* was built with several different compartments in its hull to make it "unsinkable." The theory behind this is sound. If the ship develops a major leak in one compartment, the water will be confined and won't flow into other parts of the ship.

The Titanic had a major design flaw: Those compartments were not sealed; they were too short and didn't extend all the way to deck level. So when water eventually filled one compartment, it simply flowed over into the next one, and eventually filled it. On and on this continued, until the ship sank. The damage to one small part of the ship ended up destroying the whole ship.

The same thing happens in our relationships. If we don't compartmentalize that little issue or that little destructive conversation, and if we let it flow outside that containment area to other areas, it has a tendency to disrupt our balance and our focus and our emotions—and it can seep into every aspect of our life, and our partner's life.

Compartments need to be airtight. Build them to the top.

My wife and I do this by scheduling time on a weekly basis to discuss important issues. We air important issues during this time, so they don't spill over into other areas of our life, such as our date night or other times when we're enjoying each other's company.

Compartmentalizing issues and conflicts doesn't always mean you're going to resolve them in a short time frame. But it's cathartic when you talk about them, get them out of your system, and then know they won't be a cancerous force that lingers and grows because, while you're dealing with them, you're *keeping them in their place*.

IT ALL GOES BACK TO CLARITY

The number one reason we suffer from junk and the clutter in our lives? I believe it's lack of clarity. When you're not clear, you tend to be indecisive; you tend to vacillate between the course of action you should take to accomplish goals in all areas of life, and courses of action (or inaction) that won't yield those results. You're not clear on what direction to go, so you don't make a decision. This tends to create clutter, and it tends to create junk that we drag with us. We get bogged down. Sometimes, this indecision is a function of "paralysis by analysis." We sit there and look at many options, overanalyze each of them, and end up doing nothing.

The reason, always, is that you're not clear on what you want to accomplish. So you do things (or don't do things) that have consequences, and the byproduct of this is junk and clutter. Clarity of intention leads to clarity in action, and that generates much less junk as a byproduct.

THE BLESSING—AND CURSE—OF TECHNOLOGY

A major area of distraction for most people I work with involves technology. It's a major cause of clutter—which is ironic as it's supposed to help keep us organized. In theory and promise, technology was supposed to help us do things faster, so we'd have a greater quantity of time and more quality time. But the reality is that technology has made us available 24/7. **We are working more because we're available more.**

Statistics show that we are actually 17 percent less productive because we're so busy dealing with junk and clutter—and demands—created by technology.

Email is one of the biggest culprits. It is one of the foremost low-payback activities (I'll give more details on this soon) and the cause of many big mistakes we commit.

During my speaking engagements, I often walk up to an audience member with a piece of paper and say, "Here's a memo; I need an answer to this. I need an answer *right now*. I need you to respond to it right now." They'll look at me with a puzzled expression. Then I say, "Pretend there are 25 people standing behind me, each holding a piece of paper, each of them needing an answer from you *right now*."

Would you tolerate that? Never. If you were forced to tolerate it, you'd go crazy.

In effect, that's email.

When people email you, your brain cannot help but react. You will immediately open the email, or at least look to see who sent it and read the subject line. You'll stop what you're doing, losing productivity and focus, and—9 times out of 10—you'll be dealing with somebody else's agenda at that immediate moment, instead of focusing on what you need to do to be most productive.

I know we all need to deal with email, and some emails are high-priority. But your goal should be to deal with email on *your* terms, not somebody else's.

How to accomplish that? Have specific times when you check your email and respond to emails. During the rest of the time, **keep your email program closed**. Put your mobile device away, or turn off the email function. Get it out of your peripheral vision so it won't distract you from doing the things that you need to do. Follow this advice and you will stay clear and focused on the objectives that you need to deal with. You'll stay intentional on your own high-priority tasks instead of dealing with somebody else's stuff.

Those "urgent" emails you might miss? Believe me, if it's truly urgent, they'll connect with you.

JUST IN CASE

What are the three words that cause more junk and clutter than the rest of the dictionary contents, combined?

Just. In. Case.

We often don't let go of junk because we think it may—may—benefit us to have it down the road. We will hold onto a relationship, a job, and countless material things "just in case" we end up wishing we had them. We don't want to regret getting rid of them…especially if we fear that we won't be able to replace them.

This is the scarcity mentality. And it's deeply rooted in the "just in case" scourge.

"I know this might not be the best relationship for me, but what if I can't find another person like her?"

"I know this job isn't the best fit, but what if I quit and I can't get another one?"

"I've had this thing sitting in my basement for 20 years, and I could really use the space. But what if I get rid of it and then wish I had kept it later?"

"I better just leave things alone. For now. Just in case."

Simply stated, the scarcity mentality sets in when you're afraid that there's not something better out there then what you already have, even though what you already have is not benefiting your life. You may know you need a better relationship, a better job, but until you become intentional and take action to pursue it, it will seem worthwhile to stick with the non-satisfying situation you have.

It's all too easy to spell out the solution: You need to let go of the past, and let go of the things in the present that aren't working for you.

If you're an American, you live in the most abundant country on the face of this planet. Even in the worst of times, there is so much opportunity, so much creativity and so many resources around us, having a scarcity mentality is completely illogical. There are oceans of opportunities for you to pursue your goals. But you'll never do it if you're holding on to the status quo out of fear.

IF THERE'S A MIST IN THE PULPIT THERE'LL BE A FOG IN THE PEW

I first heard this bit of wisdom a long time ago, and I think it's an apt description of how even a tiny failure of clarity from the leaders can degenerate into total confusion among those being led. If the person in a leadership role doesn't have clarity, that confusion will filter down to everybody else—and multiply in severity.

This same principle is at work when you have even a minor lack of clarity in your own purpose. By the time your thoughts translate into actions that lack of clarity will multiply in severity. A small amount of *inner* clutter and confusion can lead to illogical, aimless actions that seem wholly confused.

JUNK INSIDE, JUNK OUTSIDE (AND VICE VERSA)

To put it in very simple terms, the junk that we're carrying on the inside will eventually show up as junk on the outside. And vice versa: If our physical surroundings are bogged down with junk, we'll end up with the junk on the inside.

Having clarity reduces the junk in your life, because you are able to say, "I do need this, but I *don't* need that. I do need to work on this relationship, but I *don't* need to work on that one."

Of course, not everything we put aside is truly junk. Often our "go" or "no-go" decisions involve two options that are each viable. Any choice we make to pursue something or someone tends to also be a choice (sometimes inadvertent) to *not* pursue something or someone else. And this can cause what I call "values conflict," resulting in a mental tug-o-war.

Two options are competing with each other, because we don't have time or resources (or we know it isn't fair) to pursue both of them. Then, given a lack of clarity, and a lack of clear priorities, we don't know how to resolve the conflict. "These are both important," the brain says. "So which do I pursue? Which do I neglect?"

Here's the classic mental tug-o-war:

"It's important for me to be at work and put in the extra time so I get promoted, but it's also important for me to be home with my family."

Other times, it can be much simpler: "I want to do this, but I know I really shouldn't," you may think subconsciously.

This is when paralysis and procrastination often kick in. The tug-o-war becomes a stalemate. Inaction becomes your path. The answer is to push for greater clarity and assign a finer priority scale to your values. You probably already know which choice deserves priority, and which path you should take. If you have clearly defined, written goals, they will give you the answer. If being a more attentive father is one of your top goals, and getting a promotion is one of your bottom three goals, you'll have your answer.

Having clarity doesn't remove all discomfort surrounding your decision and next steps. Many choices are interrelated. But at least you won't be the person who lacks clarity and, at any given time, doesn't know which path or action is *truly* the most important one to take based on their individual goals and desires.

GETTING RID OF THE JUNK

So how do we deal with the junk?

When I work with clients I try to get them to identify a major clutter project for every 90 day period, then a couple of smaller ones that they know they can knock out right away. If you chip away at the junk and clutter in your life for a short period each day, you will soon achieve an amazing sense of freedom.

You can also commit a full day to the cause. This may be especially helpful if you are working on a clutter-removal project with your partner.

Whether it's a little bit of time each day, or a lot of time all at once, committing and starting are the two biggest parts of the equation. Make this a written goal! Just knowing that you have a plan of action to deal with junk and clutter will help you to stay focused.

There are countless ways you can attack clutter. Here are a few examples of sample clutter projects that clients have performed:

- Catch up on incomplete filing. You can set up or streamline the home filing system, or you can update your will or estate plan. One of the best gifts I ever gave my wife and family? I made a complete list of all of our financial and accounting information. Included in the list was the location of my will, contact information for my attorney, the location of all our financial assets and who the contact people are in each location.

- Organize family pictures into digital photo albums, and create annual family video highlights.

- Clean out and organize a garage or an attic—or just start with a single drawer. Do something!

- Set up an automatic payment for recurring bills. That's something I put off for the longest time and now I pay all my bills electronically. It's an incredible timesaver and paper saver. Plus, I'm more organized at the end of the fiscal year, personally and professionally, as I have an accounting and a summary of all my bills.

- Create a nutritionally healthy house, which only contains the food and drinks that support a high-energy and nutritional lifestyle (see chapter 1).

- Schedule time with people you have been meaning to invest time with.

- Make reservations for your annual physical to make sure you're in shape for peak performance.

- Take action on overdue acts of appreciation. Write somebody a letter and let them know how much you appreciate them.

- Back up or store key computer files. I have an external hard drive for my computer, for just this purpose. If your computer died tonight and all the files on your hard drive were gone, what would happen? If that's too scary to contemplate, back it up *today*!

- Reach out to restore a weakened or damaged friendship or other relationship.

THREE QUESTIONS TO IDENTIFY JUNK

Not certain if it's junk? Asking yourself these questions will help you get a clear idea of where the real junk in your life is located.

1. What situation or circumstance is disrupting your peace of mind? It's a question I ask every business owner and every CEO of the companies I work with. What keeps you up at night? I remind them that the issues keeping us up at night are the issues we're not dealing with during the day. We're letting them sit there as mental clutter.

2. What do you need to start doing, and what do you need to stop doing? This puts a finer point on identifying the things that are helping and hurting you. Now that you've identified them, which are you going to pair to the immediate *actions* of starting and stopping?

3. Are there areas of your life where you are not being honest with yourself? Are you pretending that everything is OK in your personal or professional life when it really isn't? I can't tell you how many people I meet that pretend they have their lives "all together." They want to create the outside perception that their relationships are doing great, their finances are in

good standing, and they have no big concerns. But you'll find something quite different when you take the time to really talk with them, to really dig deep, as I've mentioned before.

And by "dig deep," I'm certainly not talking about prying into their personal lives without invitation or hunting for dirt or gossip to share with other people. I'm talking about investing the time to find out where they're hurting and help them. You may learn that they were not being honest with themselves and putting up a front in order to cope with an extremely stressful situation. I have found when you take the time to talk with people; you will find that everyone has a story. They've got something significant that they're dealing with. Remember, the first step in eliminating junk is identifying it and then taking action to deal with it.

As "junk" is really a catch-all for an almost countless variety of specific psychological issues that can prevent people from accomplishing the most meaningful goals in their life, the information in this chapter really only scratches the surface in trying to address this thorny, universal topic. I recommend seeking more information if you want to gain a broader understanding. Of course, a mental health expert can be of immense help. Finally, I co-created a CD series entitled *Success Is Not an Accident, Secrets of the Top 1%,* that offers more tips to identify and eliminate specific types of junk. For more information, please go to www.VitalVisionsInc.com.

80-20 PRINCIPLE

Just as prioritizing is vital to eliminating junk, having a reliable formula you can apply to all your decision-making is extremely valuable.

Remember the **80/20 Principle** from Chapter Four? It's so valuable, and so accurate, it's worth spending the effort to get a full understanding of how it works.

The Pareto Principle, or **The Strength Principle,** or the **80/20 Principle** basically states that **20 percent of our efforts create 80 percent of our productivity,** in all realms of life. Restated, 20 percent of our time, effort and energy are responsible for creating 80 percent of the results we reap.

This is true in business, in relationships, and just about anything you can apply it to. It's actually been proven scientifically and statistically to hold true in many situations. For example, 20 percent of your clients will generate 80 percent of your gross revenue. If you're making sales calls, 20 percent of your calls will generate 80 percent of your successful sales. If you're running a company, 20 percent of your employees will be responsible for 80 percent of your company's income. Dropping 20 percent of your most problematic, time-consuming vendors will free up 80 percent of the time you spend dealing with vendors in general. In a relationship, 20 percent of the actions you take create 80 percent of the positive results you're looking for. On and on it goes.

When you identify the key 20 percent that's directly responsible for so much of your success (or your trouble), you have a very powerful opportunity to use **The Pareto Principle.** If you can identify the 20 percent of your clients or customers who are giving you 80 percent of your revenue, and focus on that 20 percent of your client base, think of all the time, effort and energy you could save by cutting back on your low-yield clients—the 80 percent of your clients who only generate 20 percent of your revenue!

Think about that again. **What would happen if you just focused your time, effort, and energy on the** *20 percent* **of your customers that generated** *80 percent* **of the income or revenue to your business?**

To get a very good grasp on **The Pareto Principle,** I highly recommend that you read *Living the 80-20 Way,* by Richard Koch. Here's an excerpt from his book:

> *As you simplify your life, you'll notice many positive changes. Living the simple life means less things done out of a sense of duty and more done for fun and recreation. Living the simple life means less routine and more surprises. Living the simple life means less activities with a low return on your energy and more activities with a high return on your energy. Living the simple life means less time waiting or worrying and more time enjoying what you do. Living the simple life means seeing less of the people you don't like and more of seeing the good friends and people you do like. Living the simple life means less going to the places you don't like and more of going to the places you do like. Living the simple life means less phone calls and more time to think. It means less travel and commuting and more peace and quiet. It means less driving and more walking and cycling. It means less exercise you don't like and more exercise you do like. It means fewer crises in your life and more thinking about how to avoid crises in your life. It means less taking the rough with the smooth and more taking the smooth with the smooth. It means less information overload and more information of specific and special interest. It means less spending and more giving away and recycling. It means fewer habits you don't enjoy very much and more daily rituals you love. It means less big things that make a little difference and more little things that make a big difference.*

THE SIMPLE LIFE

Here's an exercise that can help you simplify your life and live an uncluttered, junk-free existence:

1. Describe the most ideal "simple life" for you. How does it differ from the life you are living today?

2. Do you really think it's possible "to get more with less?" If so, what gives more in your life? What gives less?

3. What negative things in your life consume the most energy but give little, if anything, in return?

4. If you had to abandon one current project, challenge or goal or dream that has been chronically stalled, which one would you choose to remove and why? And then how could you reallocate the energy and focus that you were using on that stalled project to move in the direction you want to go?

Don't let the junk that life throws at you drag you down. Don't let it prevent you from accomplishing everything you were meant to do and from becoming the person you were meant to be. Apply the principles and tactics in this chapter, and you will find that you truly can remove the junk and clutter from your life. Now go make it happen.

CHAPTER 7:

RESPECT THE POWER OF EXPOSURES

"Be around the people you want to be like, because you will be like the people you are around."

SEAN REICHLE

One day shortly after she'd graduated from Columbia University, my daughter Courtney came home from work and asked me, "Dad, how do you maintain your integrity and still manage to have all of the business success that you have?"

She asked this because she saw some people she worked with cutting corners and doing things that didn't demonstrate integrity. Also, in the news at that time, there were several examples of CEOs who took short cuts and ended up costing their company millions of dollars, due to business practices that were less than legal, moral and ethical. Greed got to them and they took paths that caused the demise of themselves and, in some cases, their companies.

I answered my daughter by recounting the following story.

As far back as I can remember, I always wanted to be in business for myself. And after graduating from college and getting fired from my first three jobs it became apparent that I would have to be self-employed. The first business opportunity I pursued was in the sporting goods industry. It involved one of the first mall-concept sporting goods retailers—a company headquartered in Hollywood, Florida.

Its two principles were growing their company from one store to about 40 stores by bringing in a family member or a good friend to be their partner and the owner/manager at each specific site around the country. I was the first recruit who was not a friend or a family member. Nothing so special about me—they simply ran out of friends and relatives they could use as partners. I started working for them in a small store in Daytona Beach and increased store sales by 150 percent in 18 months. My formula was a simple one: I was always there, I gave great customer service and I managed the operation conscientiously.

Without realizing it, all along I was being taught by the people who owned these stores about how to run them and how they did business. I call it the "Ferrari Syndrome," and it works like this: "If you do as I say and play by our rules, you too can have a 308 GTI Ferrari written off on the business." Both of the principle owners had such cars, and you know what? I fell for it hook, line and sinker. I wanted a red Ferrari. I found out that "playing by their rules" meant that I had to break everybody else's rules in order to get that Ferrari.

That's how I learned what *not* to do in business, and I promised myself that when I had my own company I would do things the right way, the legal way and the moral way, and surround myself with the right people. You maintain your integrity by surrounding yourself with the right people and by doing what's right regardless of the circumstances. *What's wrong is wrong no matter who is for it, and what's right is right no matter who is against it.*

LIFTING UP VS. PULLING DOWN

I have a dear friend, Lowery Robinson, who tells a story about speaking to a group of young children. He asked a young girl to come forward to the edge of the stage and give him her hand and just stand there. Lowery used to play professional baseball and was a very fit guy. He tried to pull this young girl up onto the stage with him, but he pulled with all his might and he couldn't do it. Then Lowery said to the young girl, "I want you to grab my hand, and try to pull me down off the stage." Sure enough, she gave one tug and down he came. He turned to the group and said, "It's just like that in life. It's hard to lift people up to your standards and expectations, and it's easy for them to pull you down to theirs."

THERE IS NO NEUTRAL GROUND

The people we surround ourselves with are either lifting us up and moving us closer to our goals, or pulling us down and dragging us farther from our goals—farther from being that person that we're striving to become. There is no neutral ground on either a professional or personal level.

Obviously, that was the case with my sporting goods venture. At the time I simply didn't know any better. I was young, pursuing an opportunity to be in business for myself. I learned a lot about business there, but I also decided from then on I would always do what I call a "value add." In other words, start off with the *right values* and then *add* the business element. It means having a pre-determined idea of how to respond to any situation that arises. *If you don't pre-determine how you're going to respond in any situation, you may react to the circumstances based on what everybody else is doing, regardless of whether it's legal, moral or ethical.*

A couple I know told me a story from when their son (who's now grown) was four years old and had just finished preschool. At a conference with the teacher, they were told that their son was in a class with several disruptive boys. Now was the time to decide whether he'd stay with this class, or be held back a year—a decision that might affect him for his entire school career.

You might say, "How can someone look at a four-year-old and make that determination?"

The teacher recommended that the parents hold their four-year-old son back a year. If they didn't, he would be with these same boys for the next ten years. The class behind him, she said, had a group of children from really solid families. So the parents made the decision to hold their son back. They decided that this was the best choice for them and their son, even though it went against the norm.

Now let's fast forward. It's almost 20 years later. Four of those disruptive boys from the original class have actually been in jail, or are struggling with alcohol and drug issues. The boy who was held back a year? He has graduated from college and is currently getting his law degree. Now, there are no guarantees that his being removed from his original class was the influential factor in his current success. One can't automatically assume that he, too, would have gone to jail or struggled with substance abuse if he had remained with the original group of disruptive boys. But there's good reason to believe that his being held back a year, and spending his early childhood with a different set of peers, was an influential factor in his development.

I find it amazing that the parents recognized the potential negative impact that the association with those other boys could have on their child, and made a proactive but unconventional decision to increase his chances of success by surrounding him with a better group of people.

As a parent, you might lose count of the times you'll say to your children, "I don't want you hanging out with those people, because they're a bad influence on you." But how often do you subject the people that you associate with to the same type of scrutiny? Do they have the same values that you have? Are they lifting you up or are they pulling you down?

THE DIAMOND AND THE ROCK

My middle daughter Stefany was the first of my girls to come home from college with a boyfriend. I'll never forget that day. Dating was a big issue; our daughters didn't date until they were 16 years old.

We took Stefany and the young man to lunch and then returned to our house. As he was about to enter into our home he said, "Mr. Cesari, do you want me to remove my shoes before I come into your house?"

It was a polite request. However, I looked at him and said, "I'm going to say this one time only. As long as you're in my house, you don't take off *any* clothing, at *any* time, in *any* room." I just turned around and walked away, and my daughter was none too pleased.

Stefany dated this young fellow for almost a year. Although he was very bright, we could tell he was not lifting her up. When she came home for break by herself, I called her into the kitchen. I took a big, sparkling replica of a diamond my wife had just purchased and put it on the kitchen table. I said, "Stefany, do you know what that diamond represents?"

"No."

"That represents you. When you walk into a room you light it up, you make it sparkle. You're a diamond in the rough. You have an incredible personality that positively impacts other people."

Then I put a rock on the table and said, "Do you know what this represents?"

She said, "No."

Now, I don't want to use the young man's real name, so let's call him "Bob."

I said, "That represents Bob. Bob does not light you up. He does not help make you sparkle. And you need someone who can make you sparkle and lift you up and help you be all that you can be."

My daughter began to cry. My wife was frustrated with me for not telling her ahead of time what I was going to do. But, to this day, my daughter says, "Dad that was one of the most important things you ever did in my life."

When I asked her if I could share the story in this book she said, "Yes, because I learned such an important, valuable lesson, and I really want other people to learn it too."

Remember, sometimes we have to bypass the rock to get to the diamond. Legendary coach Lou Holtz used to ask his potential players or potential coaching hires three questions that can transform the quality of any relationship:

- **Can I trust you?** If you can't trust the people in your life, that's a big red flag, whether it's a personal relationship or a business relationship.

- **Do you care about me?** What are the motives of your business associates and people in your personal relationships? Do they truly care about you, or are they just associating with you to get to something?

- **Are you committed to excellence?** So many people in so many companies are just committed to maintaining the status quo, to just getting by and are not really committed to continually growing on a personal and professional level.

If the answer to any one of these questions is "no," you have a problem. If you ask yourself the same questions, how would that impact the choices you make? Remember, this whole book is about clarity and making proactive decisions. Who you associate with is one of the most important factors in that quest.

THE SEVEN QUALITIES OF EFFECTIVE RELATIONSHIPS

These qualities hold true for every relationship we have. They impact us whether we are aware of them or not, so it is important that you familiarize yourself with these laws and utilize them to maximize your relationships.

1. Priority

All relationships are not of equal value. This is true both personally and professionally. So exercise great care in choosing the key alliances in your life. Distinguish between whom you can afford to spend a few minutes with and who deserves a few hours. It is your responsibility to give your time to people who are going to help lift you up. In John Maxwell's book, *Laws of the Inner Circle,* he notes that your advisors will make you or break you. Every leader ought to build an inner circle that adds value to him or her and to the organization. But choose well, for the members of this inner circle will either make you or break you.

2. Attraction

You are a living magnet. You see this so often with people in dating. People attract others who conduct their lives in a similar way, or individuals who reflect their most dominant thinking. It follows that becoming the "right person" is the fastest way to attract another right person—in dating, business, and any other area of life. Relationships are basically mirrors—they reflect the quality and level of our thinking. When you think well of yourself, for the right reasons, you're going to attract that same type of person into your life. **Remember, clarity attracts.** When you're clear about what you're looking for, you'll attract the right people and the right resources into your life.

3. Excluded alternatives

When you choose to allow somebody into your life, you almost subconsciously choose to *not* allow someone else into your life. Low-value relationships displace high-value relationships. When you're spending time with the right people, you aren't investing time with the wrong people.

Please note that when I use the term "right people," I don't mean you should be judgmental in a petty way. I'm talking about surrounding yourself with people who are going to lift you up and continually challenge you and help you grow to be the person you were meant to be. This doesn't happen by accident.

4. Association

You inevitably take on the values, attitudes, beliefs, habits, and even the body language and mannerisms of the people with whom you spend the most time.

So if you're trying to become an engineer, should you hang out with a group of attorneys? Or should you hang out with a group of engineers? If you're trying to earn $100,000 a year and are currently earning $40,000 per year, should you only hang out with people who make $40,000? My point isn't strictly about money, but rather that you naturally take on the habits, values, attitudes and beliefs of the people with whom you associate.

One of my clients is the 25th wealthiest person in the country, a multibillionaire. He thinks and acts and has habits that are different from most people, and they reflect the reason why he became a billionaire.

5. Nurturing

When you pay attention to something, it grows and expands. When you neglect something it atrophies and deteriorates. To thrive, relationships need to be nurtured. Time, effort and creativity must be summoned constantly and proactively to keep any relationship growing and flourishing.

6. Understanding

Learn all you can about your most important relationships. The more you know, the better you can serve, and the more meaningful deposits you can make and the greater the harvest you will reap. Learn what people like and what motivates them. Learn what type of gifts they like, so that you can write them a note or give them a word of encouragement or send them something that's relevant to them.

7. Accountability

Seek relationships and alliances with those who will hold you accountable to ever-higher standards of personal performance. Iron does sharpen iron. How are your primary associations encouraging you to grow? One of the common missing links in really helping people grow is holding them to a higher standard, to the values that are important in their life, and giving them the permission to tell you when you are moving away from those values yourself.

NEVER UNDERESTIMATE FATE

When I was a freshman at Northeastern University in 1972, I played football on scholarship. I had early success as a tight end on the junior varsity team. In my very first game I caught 11 passes for 97 yards. I scored a touchdown and a conversion. These stats remain a freshman record to this day.

After that first game, I was brought up to the varsity. Unfortunately, someone was already in my spot. There was a junior who played tight end on the varsity squad and he started most of that year. I practiced with the varsity but I would play in the JV games.

During my sophomore year, the tight end in front of me was a senior. Our coach said he liked to play the older players; that was his policy. During practices, I would always outperform this older player in my slot; I would out-block and out-catch him. Yet I never got to start. Most everybody on the team knew I was better football player than the senior tight end. The offensive line coach was frustrated at my lack of playing time, but the head coach stuck to his decision—the senior played and I didn't.

Our fourth game of the season was against the University of Rhode Island. I sat on the bench as usual and started getting some *stinkin' thinkin'* and a bad attitude. I was at college on a full scholarship but I was ready to walk away due to my frustration at not playing. Quitting the team meant I would probably lose my scholarship, and without that scholarship money I would have to drop out of college.

I was frustrated. I was discouraged. I was ready to quit and give up.

But something happened in that game that changed my life. About two minutes before halftime, the senior tight end ran across the middle to catch a pass and took an incredible blow to his midsection. He got knocked out of the game. We didn't know it at the time, but the blow had ruptured his spleen and he was out for the rest of the season.

Although it happened under extremely negative circumstances—the injury of a fellow player—I finally had my chance. I played the whole second half and gave my best effort. I didn't do anything spectacular. I caught a few passes and made some nice blocks.

But after the game, the Rhode Island defensive end who played against me came up to me and he said, "I can't believe that you're not starting." He said, "In the first half of the game I totally owned the tight end that was in here. But in the second half you owned me; you beat me on just about every play."

I looked back and smiled, and said, "Thanks. You see that guy over there, the head coach? Can you go tell him what you just told me?"

I had never met this guy before. All he did was walk over and give me a few words of praise and encouragement. But it literally turned my life around. In that instant, I stopped my *stinkin' thinkin'*. All thoughts of quitting were gone from my head after this short exchange—even though I still expected to be back on the bench the next game, as no one knew the senior tight end's injury was season-ending.

I kept my place on the first string for the rest of that season, and was the starting tight end for the next two years. I think about how close I came to giving up. If that tight end hadn't been injured, and I didn't change my *stinkin' thinkin'*, I could have walked away from a full scholarship and dropped out of college. But due to a hard tackle and a few words of encouragement from a stranger, I completed my education and had a great college football career.

BEING A CEO (CHIEF ENCOURAGEMENT OFFICER)

In their book *How Full is Your Bucket?*, Tom Rath and Donald O. Clifton, PhD, suggest that people are either *bucket fillers* or *bucket dippers*. Is your spouse, your best friend, your co-worker or even a stranger filling your bucket by making you feel more positive? Or do they dip from your bucket, leaving you more negative than before?

Even the briefest interactions affect your relationships, your productivity, your health and your longevity. I just want to share a few of the statistics that came from *How Full is Your Bucket?*, because I think they're absolutely incredible. If you can use these lessons in your personal and business life, it will revolutionize your relationships and the way you look at people and the way other people look at you.

- The number one reason people leave their jobs is that they don't feel appreciated. A study found that negative employees can scare off every customer they speak with for good. Nine out of ten people say they are more productive when they are around positive people. The magic ratio is that it takes five positive interactions to counter one negative interaction, whether you're talking to your children, your spouse or someone at work. Remember, people crave appreciation almost as much as they do financial compensation.

- A negative boss can increase your likelihood of having a stroke by 33 percent. On the other hand, increasing positive emotions in others could lengthen your lifespan by up to ten years.

"Appreciate everything your associates do for the business; nothing else can quite substitute for a few well-chosen, well-timed, sincere words of praise. They are absolutely free and worth a fortune."

WAL-MART FOUNDER SAM WALTON

Every company and organization that I speak to has what I call an "energy troll," or that person who walks into a room and immediately sucks the energy out of it no matter how positive the meeting has been. That's why we all need to be the **Chief Encouragement Officers (CEOs)** wherever we work. We need to encourage those around us by showing honest, sincere appreciation.

This begs the question, of course, who is your CEO? Who lifts you up? Who encourages you? The most successful people in business and in life are those who offer encouragement and sincere appreciation to people they come in contact with every day, beginning at home. Outstanding leaders go out of their way to boost the self-esteem of their personnel. "If people believe in themselves it is amazing what they can accomplish," said Sam Walton.

I have a good buddy named Dave who really exemplifies this. I met Dave on a plane coming back from Arizona where I had addressed 300 medical salespeople. He paid a compliment to me and my wife as we were standing on the plane, and I really felt uplifted. Dave shared a story with me that back in the days of Eastern Airlines, before the airline industry really tightened up; he would buy a single rose in the airport for a few dollars and give it to the female attendant in charge of ticketing. Then he would say, "You are a first class person, and so am I, but you know what? Today they've stuck me in coach. Is there any way you can move me up front?"

Eighty percent of the time he got a free upgrade for the price of a rose and a sincere compliment.

I'm not suggesting that you have an agenda or expectation when you pay someone a compliment, but it will always make the other person feel special, and that person will naturally want to help you.

I recently met with the CEO (chief executive officer, in this case) of Dave's company in Oklahoma City, and you know what else I found out about Dave? He's the number one salesperson and producer in the company. Do you think that's an accident? I don't.

When I was returning from Oklahoma City, I arrived at the airport early and decided to try Dave's tactic of a flower and a sincere compliment. The only problem was that when I got up to the counter there was a male attendant. I struck up a conversation anyway, paid him a sincere compliment, and he started asking me about Atlanta. He was seeking more culture than where he lived, in Oklahoma City. We talked for maybe five minutes since no one was in line behind me.

When we were done talking, I said, "Gosh, is there any room in first class? I'd love to have the room to spread out on the way back." He put me on a list, and by the time I got to the gate, I'd been approved for first class. It just goes to show, when you appreciate other people, they want to return the favor.

Becoming a CEO at home is important, too. It's easy to be negative and point out when our children or our spouse are doing something wrong that annoys us. Instead, find them doing something right and praise them for it.

Ask yourself these questions: Who in your life needs to hear sincere appreciation? Is it your spouse, one of your children, a co-worker, or your boss? We all have daily opportunities to impact somebody in a positive way, to serve them, to encourage them, to show sincere appreciation. My challenge to you is to find somebody doing something right at home, at work, or even in the community, and praise them for it. Doing so can transform a life; it can transform a relationship; it can re-energize a business.

POSITIVE MENTAL NUTRITION

Positive mental nutrition is the deliberate, productive input that comes from what you read, watch or listen to. Just as with people, **there is no neutral ground** in this regard. The information you consume is either lifting you up or dragging you down.

We all need a healthy mind as much as a healthy body, a mind that will work for us instead of against us. A healthy mind keeps your attention on your intention, and stores up goal-directed thoughts as opposed to fear-based thoughts.

What can you do to achieve a healthy, disciplined mind? You can start by being intentional about what you expose it to. Most people just absorb things as they happen. They listen to whatever is playing on the TV or radio; they read whatever's printed in the daily newspapers; they read the books that everybody else is reading. They take a very casual and reactive approach to what they are feeding their minds, just as many take the same low-end approach to feeding their bodies.

While it's important to keep in touch with what is going on in the world, you don't need to feed your brain all the negative junk now offered in the media. We are bombarded with more information than at any other time in our history. And the question is, how do you discern what is truth, what is garbage and what is healthy and nutritious for your mind? I like what Zig Ziglar says about this: **"Every morning when I wake up I read the Bible, and then I read the paper; that way I can keep track of what both sides are doing."**

The most successful people I know closely monitor what they let into their minds.

When you put garbage into your body, you pay the unpleasant short-term and long-term consequences. When you allow garbage into your mind, you clog your potential for satisfaction and lasting success. I used to think it was just garbage in, garbage out; but now I've realized that the garbage we let in our minds stays there. Our subconscious mind retains the junk and retrieves it later. When you put the right positive mental nutrition into your mind then good, positive benefits come out.

GET YOUR POSITIVE MENTAL NUTRITION IN BED

Pay very close attention to what you allow into your mind during the 15 minutes before you go to sleep. The stimuli we receive at bedtime can determine whether we wake up with a positive, can-do attitude or wake up with *stinkin' thinkin'.* If you tune into the 11 o'clock news before you go to bed, you'll hear a rundown of all the crises around the world. You'll hear about murders and rapes. And you'll go to bed with that in your subconscious. I believe that it can alter the quality of your sleep, affect your dreams and cause you to wake up with a negative outlook. Instead, read something positive. I often read Bible verses, but anything uplifting will do.

To live an exceptional life you must deliberately immerse yourself in inspiring and uplifting thoughts. You must capture the hidden opportunities and spare moments and surround yourself with positive mental nutrition. Everything you read and everything you watch and listen to, impacts your character and personality. As a result, directly or indirectly, it influences every decision you make.

Your television can be a great source of negative stimuli, even if you only keep it on in the background without attentively watching it. My wife and I once made a New Year's commitment to turn off the TV for a month. We were amazed how it automatically opened up the door for so many other positive things to occur, because your mind searches for things to occupy the time you waste watching TV. We spent more quality time together. I read more books in one month than I had read the previous year.

When our children were young, we had a rule in our home that they could watch a half hour of TV for every hour of reading they did. It made watching TV a reward, and even then we were very selective and intentional with what we allowed them to watch. You need to take the same perspective for yourself. Don't allow yourself to take in information accidentally. Look for things that are inspiring, from faith to fitness to marriage to parenting.

POSITIVE SELF-TALK

I once went to Canada to launch a new line of supplements on The Shopping Channel. I was well prepared for it, having spent lengthy prep time with a mentor. I rehearsed in front of him before I made the trip, and on my own I rehearsed in front of the mirror repeatedly. I had about eight minutes on camera to make several pitches. The first spot was at 6:30 a.m., and I thought I nailed it. I came out of there pumped. Immediately afterward in the green room I could see the sales numbers as they registered on a monitor. My brilliant presentation had sold *two* bottles of supplements. Typically, they want you to average between $10,000 and $25,000 each time you go on air.

I sold $50 worth of product.

I felt like a loser. My confidence fell from the mountaintop to the valley floor. I went back in to my dressing room and started packing my bag to go home. I was supposed to go back out there six more times over the course of the next ten hours, about once every 90 minutes, but now I was scared to death. I didn't want to go back out and humiliate myself again.

I called my partner, Tommy, back in Atlanta, and thank goodness he picked up the phone. Tommy is very gifted at helping people through tough situations. I explained everything that had happened. His response: "Steve, you're going to talk yourself back into success. Get a pen and paper and write this down:

> *I am ready. I have an important message to deliver today. I instantly connect with my audience. My voice is strong, smooth and pleasing to hear. I smile a lot. I turn all conditions to my advantage. I am calm and poised when I speak. I radiate confidence, competence and conviction when I speak. I am focused like a laser. I've got what it takes and more for this engagement. I feel ten feet tall when I speak. I love to be bold and take charge. I have a commanding presence. I have boundless self-confidence. I am turbocharged. I energize and inspire my audience. My mannerisms are appropriate and effective. My mind is quick, sharp, and alert. I am powerful, persuasive and entertaining and charismatic. I have perfect command of the*

English language. I speak clearly and passionately. My open is strong and dazzling. Perfect and powerful words flow to me effortlessly, right when I need them. I have lots of fun in front of groups. I know my stuff. I know more about teamwork and peak performance than 99.9 percent of the population. I ask powerful and provocative questions when I speak. I am in complete command of my material and my audience."

I gave myself that talk and took the *stinkin' thinkin'* out of my mind. In the next segment, I sold $23,000 worth of product, and in the following five I averaged the same. And to think I almost left because I bombed the first time out!

Among the most powerful influences on your character, personality and attitude is what you say to yourself and what you believe. **At every single moment of every day, you're either talking yourself into or out of success.** Think about it: What are you saying to yourself about yourself? You are constantly redefining and reinventing yourself and your future with every thought in your mind. It's a scientific fact that we continually talk to ourselves and this inner dialogue or self-talk must be controlled if you are to maximize your full potential.

So what is self-talk? Simply put, it's every thought that either moves you toward your goals or away from your goals. No thoughts are neutral; every thought counts, just like the people we let into our lives.

Unfortunately, about 90 percent of the thoughts most of us have today are repeats from yesterday and the day before and the day before that. *This is the main reason why making a permanent, positive improvement in your life tends to be such a challenge.* The human mind loves the status quo; it loves the comfort zone; it loves the *known*. If not trained to do otherwise, it will feed you a constant repetition of old ideas. And those old thoughts, like an automatic pilot, will keep you steering your life in the same direction that it's always gone.

DOES YOUR PAST EQUAL YOUR FUTURE?

What you have done matters far less than *where you are going*. Your past does not equal your future—unless you make it so. If you constantly identify with current or prior performance, where you are and where you are going will be one and the same. Then your past *will* equal your future.

This holds true for your golf game, your business, your career, your marriage and every other area of your life. Imagine some part of your life that you'd like to improve. It can be anything. Since this area causing dissatisfaction is below your standards, you consider yourself to be in a ditch, far beneath your potential. It doesn't matter *how* you got in the ditch, only that you're aware of being there.

The first rule of getting out of a ditch? *Stop digging.*

In order to get out, you have to think up, look up, speak up, and, ultimately climb up. Most people have difficulty climbing out of the ditches in their lives simply because they focus more on the ditch, which represents their current circumstances, than on where they want to climb, which is the goal or the solution.

WHAT DO YOU SAY TO YOURSELF ABOUT YOURSELF?

In order to get something different, you have to do something different. And it all begins with telling yourself that you can do it. Remember, your self-talk tends to work against you unless you are aware of it and use it for your own goals and ambition. Positive self-talk is a thought you intentionally choose to think because of the results it will produce in your life. Effective self-talk is created by using what I call the PEPP formula. Specifically, effective self-talk is:

Precise and Positive

Emotion-provoking

Present tense

Personal

Let's look at each of these four qualities in detail.

Precise and Positive

Use specific, precise, positively-phrased language in your self-talk. Say "I am reading for one hour every evening," rather than, "I am no longer wasting my evening watching TV." Instead of "I am not eating ice cream," say, "I am eating only low-fat, nutritious foods."

Emotion provoking

Your self-talk should be emotion-provoking, causing you to pre-live the experience. As I mentioned before, my son was a field goal kicker. In a conversation once with the fine NFL kicker, John Kasay, my son heard the following: "Matthew, if you're going to really do this in high school and want to do it in college, you have to realize that you're going to make some and you're going to miss some, and that when you miss you just need to blow it off and walk away, and come back and do it again the next time. You have to kick a 50-yard field goal in your head before you can kick one in a game. You have to convince yourself that you can do it in your mind before you can do it on the field." Matthew has applied this concept to other parts of his life from becoming an

Eagle Scout, to his recent career choice, to growing into a man of high character and integrity. **If you can see yourself achieving it in your mind, you can make it happen in reality.**

There's an oft-told story that the actor Jim Carrey. Before he became a star, he wrote a check in the amount of $10 million payable to himself. He visualized that someday, someone was going to pay him that much for his gifts and talents. He actually achieved making that $10 million because he believed it in his head before it happened in reality.

Present Tense

Like your goals, your self-talk should always be in the present tense. The subconscious mind, where permanent change becomes rooted, does not understand or acknowledge the past or the future; it operates only in the here and now. You can affect subconscious change only by communicating in the language of the present tense.

When you affirm your goals and dreams as if they're already attained, you make the shift from being bogged down in reality to being a visionary. Remember the most powerful words in the English language are those that come after the words "I am…" Thoughts such as, "I am responsible for my thoughts" and "I am relaxed and poised, even when others are not," are mighty indeed.

Here's a sample list of present tense, positive self-talking points:

- I am responsible
- I discipline my mind
- I experience maximum energy
- I am clear about my goals
- My thoughts, words and actions are positive
- I think I can, I know I can

- I plan ahead
- I let go of junk
- I take action now
- I am ready
- I practice gratitude
- I am centered and focused
- I am honest with myself and with others
- I see the big picture
- I develop simple, effective rituals

I get lifted up just speaking those words. Even if you're not doing the actions mentioned, you'll be lifted up by just saying the words.

Personal

Self-talk is most effective when it is personal to your life and your goals. You need to make up your own list and personalize it toward your own goals. The more you positively pump yourself up, the better chance you'll achieve the goal. I use my list before I give a talk. I tell myself about the outcome I want to achieve, and I achieve it in my mind and convince myself I've already done it before I even begin.

Whenever negative talk intrudes, I replace it with a positive thought or a Bible verse. The first thing you need to do when you experience *stinkin' thinkin'* is to put a positive affirmation into your mind.

When you surround yourself with encouraging, uplifting people and fill your mind with positive mental nutrition on a daily basis, and then constantly reinforce your goals with positive self-talk, you will become an unstoppable force.

CHAPTER 8:

CREATE A "WOW" EXPERIENCE

"There is only one boss. The customer. And he can fire
everybody in the company from the chairman on down,
simply by spending his money somewhere else."

SAM WALTON

If you're a basketball fan, you may remember the excitement back in late June and July of 2010, when 2009 MVP LeBron James prepared to make a major announcement to reveal the team he would go to via free agency. The media and the fans could barely stand the tension in waiting for his decision. Will he stay in Cleveland or go to Miami, Chicago or New York? Everyone from the President of the United States on down gave their opinion on where the man simply known as LeBron should go. The excitement hit a fever pitch on Thursday, July 9—which was termed "Decision Day" by the media.

To unveil the decision, LeBron and the people who advise him decided to hold a one-on-one live interview on ESPN at 9 p.m. on July 8th. After being briefly interviewed by ESPN's Jim Gray, LeBron let the whole sports world hold its breath in the final moments before his announcement: He then told the nation that he would leave the Cleveland Cavaliers and sign with the Miami Heat.

In announcing his decision in this manner, James created one of the biggest media events in the history of sports, even though it was quite brief. (If you're not a sports fan, please take my word for it—this was a *very* big deal.)

In my opinion, it was a brilliant way to create what I call a **WOW experience.**

LeBron had 30 million people tuning in to learn his decision during the live interview. He and ESPN put the National Basketball Association brand squarely in the limelight. What's more, there was a philanthropic angle. LeBron sat for the interview and made the announcement from the Boys & Girls Club of Greenwich, Connecticut—and ESPN pledged to give the advertising and sponsorship proceeds to support the Big Brothers and Big Sisters program (a charity James regularly supports).

This is what I call a win-win-win proposition. It helped LeBron promote himself (and, to be sure, he received scathing criticism from some people—especially disappointed Cleveland fans—who considered his live prime-time announcement the height of narcissism). It helped his commercial flagship, the NBA, and it helped the Big Brothers and Big Sisters program.

So, let's re-cap the benefits from this win-win-win experience. First, LeBron won. He whetted public appetite for his product, pro basketball. Secondly, the NBA won. And thirdly, the customers, NBA fans, won—because it generated excitement for a sport they love and gave them a thrilling shared experience.

I think it was a brilliant marketing strategy. Not everyone agreed. But almost everyone can agree it qualifies as a WOW experience.

WHAT IS THE WOW EXPERIENCE?

There are three levels of effective customer service:

1. Meeting customer expectations

2. Exceeding customer expectations

3. Amazing your customers

A WOW experience is when your customers are amazed. Ideally, you want that to happen at every point of contact with your business. The purpose of business is to create and keep customers. The true measure of business success is customer satisfaction. The true measure of customer satisfaction is repeat business. Creating a WOW experience will create more repeat business.

When we started marketing the *Juiceman Juicer*, we wanted to create a WOW experience at every point of contact with our customer. While this was 16 years ago, it's more important to create a WOW experience for your customers today than it's ever been. If you don't create a WOW experience for your customers, somebody else will.

What were some of the WOW experiences we created with customers? Well, we started off the *Juiceman* business by doing free seminars, as I mentioned in an earlier chapter. We created a high-energy, informative and fun environment at all of our seminars. In addition to being entertained and informed by Jay "The Juiceman" Kordich, attendees also sampled free juice recipes that we made fresh in the back of the room.

Jay Kordich had already been selling juicers for 40 years before we got involved with him. As we conducted these free seminars, we met some people who were unhappy with Jay, due to an unpleasant experience in the past. They typically said that Jay had taken their money but not sent them a juicer, or sold them a defective juicer. So we would always have a handful of people who had done business with Jay in the past, and reported a negative experience.

We had a choice.

We could have said to them, "Well, look, we didn't own the business at that time. It's not our problem. We weren't responsible for Jay's actions or mistakes during that time."

Or, we could have decided to take responsibility and make those people happy, at our expense. And that's what we chose to do. We chose to make 100 percent customer satisfaction our corporate policy.

In the first 12 months of the business, we absorbed almost $100,000 in losses for problems we had nothing whatsoever to do with. We incurred these losses mainly by giving Jay's disgruntled customers free juicers. But our higher goal was to create a WOW experience.

Jay's past customers weren't our only issue. We had product-quality problems of our own. When we started doing business, we had what I privately called "the best of the juicers on the market." The problem was, there weren't any really good juicers at the time. Ours was one of the better products, to be sure, but it was still lacking.

We listened to what our customers were saying to us about our product at the live seminars. It was like having hundreds of focus groups a year. They told us what they liked and didn't like. As we received feedback, we would ask our manufacturers to incorporate the changes in our product. So we constantly worked on improving the quality of our juicer as we grew our business. We constantly poured revenue back into upgrading our juicers and upgrading our customer experience.

Staying in constant contact with your customer and then responding to what the customer is telling you to do is the most important thing you can do in business. Even after we stopped doing the seminars, and sold our product exclusively on television and through retailers, I would spend three hours every Friday morning sitting in the customer service department and taking phone calls to hear the problems people were having, either with the juicer or with customer service, and determining how to fix them.

A JUICER, SHOT THROUGH THE HEART

We had more than 50 customer service reps in our organization. One day, customer service received a call from a woman that had to be transferred up to me. The woman told me her son had put live ammunition—live bullets—into her juicer. And one of the bullets fired when he turned on the juicer. Thank God, nobody got hurt. But the bullet went through the motor of the juicer, and obviously this rendered it ineffective and inoperable.

The customer service person who originally fielded her call said, "Ma'am, we stand behind our product for manufacturing defects, not from abuse."

And yes, that was the policy. But whenever a phone call came to me, as the president and owner of the company, I would always go for 100 percent customer satisfaction. And this lady's problem eventually reached me.

Even though this was an extreme case, I replaced the lady's juicer.

In speaking to the woman, I said, "Ma'am, we'll be more than happy to send you a new juicer, but can I ask you a favor? Can you send us the juicer with the bullet hole through the motor? I'd like to display it here as a piece of memorabilia."

And, sure enough, she sent it in. We put it up on the wall in our customer service department as a visual reminder that we would do *whatever* was necessary to achieve 100 percent customer satisfaction.

GIVE YOUR COMPANY A CALL

Want to know if your customer service hotline or any other area of your company is delivering a WOW experience to your customers? Give your company a call. I read this once in an article, and decided to do it.

I called our company and tried to get through to customer service, and was put on hold for 11 minutes due to call volume. This seemed impossible. Not only did we have 50 customer service reps, we also had six full-time nutritionists on staff. Employing nutritionists meant our customers could call in and discuss their specific illnesses with a professional, who would offer juice recipes that offered the optimum health benefit.

We had more than enough people to answer the phones and to create a WOW experience. So when I was on hold for 11 minutes, I almost blew a gasket. I investigated the cause and dis-covered that 80 percent of our call-delay problems were caused not by our staff but by technology. Our phone system couldn't accom-modate the volume of incoming calls, even though our people could.

I met right away with our IT people to work on a solution. We developed new software—customized, not off-the-shelf—that would address our needs. It was called TOES, short for Trillium Order Entry System. Once the new system was installed our average call wait time shrank to less than one minute. Even then, we gave a caller the option to leave their name and phone number, with the promise that we would get back to them the same day (which we did).

How did this impact our bottom line? This helped us continue to grow and become one of the fastest growing privately held companies in the U.S.

This all happened because I dialed in one day on a whim. I gave my own company a call. Had I not read that article, or been busy that morning, it may have taken me many more months to learn about the call delays.

THESE DAMN CUSTOMERS

Early in my career, back in the 1980s, I worked at a sporting goods retail store called Sports Town. It was the first warehouse sporting goods concept in the marketplace. When a location came to Atlanta, I joined as general manager.

Sports Town was a 40,000-square-foot store. I had about 125 employees. Every one of them wore a button that read "Rule number one: The customer is always right." Underneath that another line read, "Rule number two: Never forget rule number one."

I hated those stupid buttons. I kept asking my bosses why, if customer service is our top priority, do we need buttons proclaiming this fact? Shouldn't our customers be able to figure it out by *how we treat them?*

Customer service begins and ends with upper management, and it has to filter through every part of the organization. It is a mindset and an attitude rather than a procedure. It's not something that you pay lip service to. It is something you ingrain into the whole corporate culture.

Well, during his calls, the senior vice president of operations would constantly remind us that customer service was our number one priority. Then, in his very next breath, he would say you need to cut payroll. He did this constantly. So we kept cutting payroll until we had about ten people covering those 40,000 square feet.

Do you know what it's like when you walk into a store and you can't find anybody to wait on you? Of course you do. We all do. Well, one day, a few of my remaining associates were stocking shelves and having a conversation, and I happened by in the next aisle. I could hear them, but they couldn't see me standing behind the shelves, so they didn't know I was there. And I'll never forget what one of them said.

"You know, we sure could get a lot of work done if it wasn't for these damn customers."

They all agreed with this statement.

I revealed myself and ask them, "Do you know who is responsible for your paychecks?"

"You are," they replied. Their paychecks read "authorized by Steve Cesari."

I said, "No, the customers are responsible for your paychecks. So if it wasn't for these damn customers, you wouldn't have a job. I wouldn't have a job. Nobody would have a job."

SAM WALTON AND WAL-MART

Sam Walton was the founder of what came to be known as Wal-Mart. A child of the Great Depression, Walton came from humble and hard-working roots. It goes without saying that he was a pioneering retailer, personally reinventing the discount general-merchandise industry in America.

Walton began his retail career in 1940 when he and his brother opened the first Wal-Mart discount store in Arkansas. Sam's shrewd business plan included cutting costs to the absolute minimum and passing savings on to the customer. He was also the first to use advanced computerization to set up automated distribution centers, a lynchpin of Wal-Mart's success.

Today, Sam's empire has grown to more than 3,000 stores and over $100 billion in revenue. Sam was a visionary. He was a pioneer. Sam knew how to create a WOW experience for his customer. Not only did he create a WOW experience, but he also created an incredible value.

OUR MISSION STATEMENT

One of the best ways to achieve clarity in an organization is to create a mission statement and corporate philosophy, and to make sure all employees know it by heart. Following is the mission statement I developed at Trillium Health Products.

The company's mission is to improve the lives of people through nutrition education and related natural health products. The basic principles which govern the company's course are a dedication to the highest in product quality, providing the latest nutrition information and preventative medicine research and exceeding our customer's expectations. And demonstrating environmental responsibility and building the organizational integration necessary to produce win-win-win results for the company's customers, suppliers and associates.

What is the mission statement of your organization? What is your corporate philosophy? What do you do on a daily basis to exceed your customers' expectations? We set out with a vision and a mission to exceed our customers' expectations—but we just didn't pay it lip service. *We took action and followed through.*

HIRING THE RIGHT PEOPLE

The WOW experience begins with hiring the right people and then taking care of them, so they, in turn, can take care of your customers, your clients or your patients.

As always, everything comes back to clarity. Our company had a clear mission to *"improve the lives of people through nutrition education and related natural health products."* Having this clarity was a paramount factor in our hiring decisions.

WE HIRE PEOPLE WHO SMILE

Someone once asked the CEO of Starbucks, "How is it you have so many employees who smile when I walk into your stores?" His answer: "We hire people who smile."

Let me illustrate why.

If the mission of your company is to climb a tree, would you rather hire a squirrel or train a horse?

Most people end up trying to train a horse to do the job. And they end up with an associate who acts like a specific part of the horse; the horse's behind. When organizations have clarity, when they have a clear vision and a mission, it makes it much easier to attract and hire the right people.

I'm working with the president of an organization right now. In discussing personnel I had him write out the specific qualifications of the employee he's looking to hire. We made this description extremely detailed. To the point that, when a job candidate is referred to the organization, or walks in to apply, it's going to be obvious whether they belong there or not.

EMPOWERING YOUR EMPLOYEES TO CREATE A WOW EXPERIENCE

It's important to empower your employees *at every level of the organization* to make decisions that will create a WOW experience for the customer. When you allow your associates to take responsibility for their results, it gives them more control over their destiny. They don't feel helpless. And the customer doesn't get frustrated.

How many times have you dealt with someone in a business who said, "I have to talk to my supervisor?" In every company that I work with, 90 percent of the decisions can be made by a frontline person who has the most direct contact with the customer. This person has a great deal of responsibility and control. When you're responsible for your results, you become an active contributor rather than a passive observer. Contributing actively allows all employees to perform better, and clears the way for the truly exceptional people to show their talents.

Why? Employees who are empowered to do whatever is necessary to achieve great results have a ready pathway to excel and to be promoted. Those who take full advantage of this will become the leaders in your organization. This starts a domino effect. A staff member takes ongoing responsibility for business results, that staff member achieves increasingly impressive goals, and others begin looking to him or her for leadership. That's why the people who take the most responsibility for their results are the people I look to promote within my organizations, as do most other business owners and leaders.

When you are responsible for your results, you gain a reputation as a problem solver. The people who solve the most problems get paid the most money, and they're worth it. Business is all about solving the problems experienced by customers and solving the organization's internal problems. People that can do that on a consistent basis provide the highest value to the operation. You must recognize this and pay them accordingly.

People who are responsible for their results experience less anger. They experience less frustration and helplessness because they are take-control types who seldom feel victimized by circumstances. This all leads to better health. And a better bottom line for both the employees and the company for which they work.

HERE'S A STORY ABOUT NOT TAKING RESPONSIBILITY

One day a farmer's donkey fell into a well. The animal cried relentlessly for hours as the farmer tried to figure out what to do. Finally, the farmer decided the animal was old and the well needed to be covered up anyway. It just wasn't worth the trouble to retrieve the donkey.

So he invited his neighbors to come over and help him. They all grabbed shovels and began to throw dirt into the well. At first the donkey realized what was happening and cried horribly. Then, to everybody's amazement, he became calm. Finally, the farmer looked down the well. He was astonished at what he saw. With each shovel of dirt that hit the donkey's back, the donkey would shake it off and take a step up.

As the farmer's neighbors continued to shovel dirt on top of the animal, he would shake it off and take a step up. Pretty soon, everyone was amazed as the donkey stepped up over the edge of the well and trotted happily off.

The donkey later came back to the farm and bit the farmer. The gash from the bite became infected and the farmer eventually died in agony with septic shock.

The moral of the story? When you do something wrong and try to cover your rear, it always comes back to bite you.

Here are a few other morals from this tale that you can share. Life is going to shovel dirt on you. If you can shake it off and take a step up, each of your troubles can be a stepping stone. We can escape the deepest wells just by never giving up, shaking it off and taking a step up.

THE TRILLIUM HEALTH PRODUCTS EMPLOYEE HANDBOOK

The text below comes directly from the employee handbook we used at Trillium Health Products, and I still use it in my business today:

We believe those who enjoy their work keep getting better at it, which makes us a more productive company. We believe individuals can learn and grow rapidly if eager to do so and surrounded by others equally anxious to learn, to teach and encourage. Because we consider people so important, we are extremely selective. Congratulations on becoming part of our team.

General expectations. Our number one goal is to provide outstanding customer service and exceed their expectation. Set both your personal and professional goals high. We have great confidence in your ability to achieve them, and we'll provide you with every possible tool to make our relationship mutually rewarding.

Customer service. We are committed to offering exceptional products and exceeding our customer's expectations. As a result, company policies and decisions are made with the customer in mind. We are confident that by listening to our customers, we can continue to expand our customer base and strengthen our position as one of the nation's leading marketers of health and nutrition products and information.

Corporate philosophy. We operate under an inverted pyramid style of management. This system exemplifies our belief that the customer always comes first. In this system, the customer is the initial source of contact influencing the decision-making process in the chain of command.

Following in importance is the sales and customer service staff, which are the direct link to the customer. The next level of the pyramid includes supervisors, managers and department heads. And then underneath them and supporting them are the officers and owners of the company.

We encourage people to be innovative in their sales technique. There is no method or procedure manual of specific selling practices. Associates are simply asked to use good judgment and accepted business practices, which are within the realm of being legal, moral and ethical.

And then, finally, we are a goal-oriented company. We encourage our associates to continually strive for and maintain high standards of performance. This quest to be the best has produced a welcome spirit of competition and camaraderie throughout the company. Associates are constantly encouraged to expand their interests physically, mentally and spiritually. Associates who join us become part of an organization where individuals are accountable for their actions and become total team players.

GOING ABOVE AND BEYOND THE CALL OF DUTY

We set high expectations for our associates, and, in turn, compensated them above industry average. It always paid off. Sure, there was the occasional exception. But for the most part, the corporate environment we created empowered and encouraged our associates to take responsibility, to take action, to go out and do whatever they had to do to exceed customer's expectations.

This resulted in some special demonstrations of associates going above and beyond what most people would think was reasonably expected of them. For example, a customer who lived two hours away from our corporate office in Seattle had a problem with her juicer. She was disabled and could not get out of her house. One of our associates suggested that he deliver the juicer personally. So he drove to her house after his work hours. He did this because he was empowered to make those types of decisions, and he was an exceptional individual. People will create WOW experiences that customers—and bosses, and everyone else—will remember forever.

CREATING VALUE

After the juicer, the next product we developed at Trillium was the Bread Man Bread Machine. It was a very good product. *Consumer Reports* rated our bread machine one of the best on the market. But we created more value by offering things customers did not expect.

For example, we were the first company to include natural whole grain bread mixes with the product. The machine came with its own bread mix, so that within 90 minutes of getting the product home, you could be eating fresh bread. You didn't have to go to the store and buy ingredients. This really differentiated the product and customers loved it.

NORDSTROM

Nordstrom, a retail company based in Seattle, is world-renowned for its customer service.

Few stories illustrate this like the one about the woman who came to a Nordstrom location and wanted to return four tires. She had a receipt, but it wasn't from a Nordstrom store. Nordstrom didn't even sell tires. But they gave this lady store credit to purchase other products.

Now, that's going to an extreme. I don't know if I would have done that in one of my businesses—and I'm a guy who replaced a juicer that was destroyed when someone put bullets in it. But Nordstrom has become world-renowned for creating the type of environment where the customers have their expectations exceeded all the time. They create a WOW experience every time you walk in the door. They train their associates to be astute in handling any sort of customer. Sure, they offer high-quality products, but they offer a great environment in which to buy them.

When I started Trillium Health Products, I adopted the "inverted pyramid" style of management, which came from Nordstrom's example. In a nutshell, the owners and executives of the organization support the managers and supervisors who support the front line associates who deal with the customers or clients every day.

When we looked at Nordstrom's inverted pyramid system, we believed it was the most direct way to create win-win-win situations in which the customer wins, our associates win and the company wins. And we believed it gave us the optimum environment for continued company growth and new opportunities for both customers and associates through the following decade. We grew from zero to $100 million in revenue in two and a half years.

THE REWARDS OF THE WOW EXPERIENCE

There are many benefits of creating a WOW experience and "going the extra mile" (a phrase I use a lot to describe creating a WOW experience). For one, you'll engender customer loyalty. When you go out of the way to exceed a customer's expectations, do you think that person is going to do business someplace else? Secondly, you'll also create extra value. That means you can normally charge more for your product or service. People are willing to pay more when they get more, and a WOW experience is more.

Another reward? The most talented people in the marketplace want to work in organizations that are creating WOW experiences. So you get a better caliber of employee seeking a position with your business. This held true in every company I've worked with. When you create an exciting environment, people want to come and work there.

Google is the epitome of this. Thousands of people want to work for Google as a result of this company creating WOW experiences. So it can pick the brightest and the best people coming out of the colleges and the universities.

Finally, industry leaders and influential parties in the marketplace notice when you're creating a WOW experience. In 1992, I received the following letter from Kenneth Kolker, who was the CEO of May Corporation, the largest conglomeration of department stores in the country at the time. He was actually congratulating me for creating a WOW experience.

Dear Steve,

Even though we haven't met, I would like to congratu-late you for conceiving and carrying out one of the greatest marketing strategies in years. As the individual who first knew and worked with Jay Kordich some 25 or more years ago, I congratulate you and your fine organization for recognizing and utilizing a unique marketing happening. Sincerely,

Kenneth Kolker

To sum it up, when you create a WOW experience, people want more of your product. They want to be connected with you. When you come out with your next product, everybody will line up to get it. And that's exactly what happened in our organization.

WHAT ARE *YOU* DOING TO CREATE A WOW EXPERIENCE?

As in, right now?

How are you differentiating yourself individually or as a company? Are you a person who goes the extra mile, takes responsibility, goes out of their way to take care of people, and adds value to their employer and to the customer every day you show up at work? What is your value proposition? Why should someone do business with you or hire you when considering all the other options available?

When you ask yourself these questions, it creates the opportunity for you to explore how you can become a more valuable member of your team or organization. If you own the business, it can help you create a greater value and empower your team to go out and exceed customer expectations. You want a top-quality product or service that offers the best possible *value*. And by that, I don't mean the lowest price.

When you live by price alone, you're going to die by price. You may face the dismal reality of seeing your product become a commodity.

You may compete and survive, but without added value, a competitor who can tolerate a lower margin will eventually wear you down.

It bears repeating: There has never been a more important time in history for you to create a WOW experience on a personal and a business level. People have too many choices now, for goods and services, and for employees. The Internet has added limitless options to these realms. So you can't be complacent. When you're in business, there are only two choices: You're either growing and playing offense and moving forward, or you're shrinking and moving backwards and becoming obsolete.

MATISHA

An example of how a business "went the extra mile" to give me a WOW experience? I was having problems with my phone, so I had to call the customer service line at a phone company in Florida. Typically, I anticipate the worst-case scenario when I have this need. I expect to be confronted with an endless maze of keypad- or voice-operated options, and then, if I do get a human, ending up with someone who doesn't care about my problem.

Well, I ended up getting Matisha as my customer service rep.

She solved my immediate problem, which satisfied my immediate need. I was gratified to have this done, even though what she provided was within the minimum expectation a customer should have. But then Matisha "went the extra mile." She looked at my billing record, and said, "You know, Mr. Cesari, we have mistakenly been billing you for two accounts for the past three years."

She researched the problem. She voluntarily went above and beyond the call of duty, and spent about 30 minutes researching and resolving a problem that I was not even aware I had. As a result, I ended up getting a tremendous refund.

When this matter was settled I sat down and, for the first time in my life, wrote a letter of appreciation to a phone company. I sent this letter to Matisha and her supervisor, and I sent Matisha a book. That's how moving the experience was for me. She went the extra mile and did something incredible that I didn't expect a phone company to do. (She didn't just exceed my expectations; she *amazed* me—and remember, that's the nucleus of all WOW experiences.)

Now, how do you think Matisha's supervisor reacted? Do you think the supervisor clearly recognized that she's a special person? What's going to happen when Matisha comes up for her review? Do you think she will be a likely candidate to be promoted, to be put in charge of more people, to teach other people how to do what she did?

I certainly hope so, and expect as much. I've certainly seen terribly run businesses in which she would have been chastised for refunding a large sum of money without being compelled to do so. But those businesses don't last long, because they are fundamentally flawed. I don't know exactly what ensued in Matisha's case due to my praising letter, but I'm willing to bet that she did very well at the company. Or she's doing very well at some other job, and her company is making more money because she's there. People who "go the extra mile" excel in the marketplace. That's a universal fact.

CREATE YOUR OWN PLAYING FIELD AND DOMINATE IT

Eric Yaberbaum is a friend and a business associate who prides himself on standing out from the pack. Eric is a PR executive and he wrote *PR for Dummies*, along with several other books. He has a simple philosophy when it comes to differentiating your company from the others.

His advice: Don't try to figure out how to capture part of an existing market. Instead, go out and create your own market. Create your own playing field and dominate it.

Eric actually worked with our company when we marketed the *Juiceman*, and his PR philosophy helped us expose our WOW experience to a lot of people. Eric was responsible for helping us deliver free seminars to 650,000 people over a period of two years. He created a PR machine that established us as experts in the health and nutrition industry and established our product as one of the best available.

I have built several successful companies using these strategies. Whether it's on a personal level or a business level, differentiating yourself from your competition is critically important. A very famous example of this follows.

THE GEORGE FOREMAN GRILL

The company that bought Trillium Health Products is the same company that launched the George Foreman Grill. My brother Rick, who's a genius at marketing (if I do say so myself, as his brother), oversaw most of the direct marketing for the George Foreman Grill.

I'll tell you, at first, *nobody* had heard of the George Foreman Grill. It was not distinct. There were already grills on the market. We didn't just want to capture part of the existing market, even though it was growing. We wanted to create a new market. The question was, how could we differentiate the George Foreman Grill to create *a different playing field* and dominate it?

I remember sitting with George Foreman and his daughter in a limousine once. I asked him, "George, what are you most passionate about?"

He said, "Oh, that's easy. I love to talk about my faith, and I love to cook, and I love to eat."

You see, the marketing message for the George Foreman Grill grew out of one of George's passions. He loved to eat, and he loved to cook. And he wasn't just endorsing a product. It was an extension of who George really is.

That was a good foundation, anyway.

My brother developed the infomercial, which opened with George Foreman in a boxing ring, wearing his robe and his heavy-weight-championship belt. The message was, "knock out the fat from your food by using my grill." Because this was the first grill that was actually elevated in the back so the grease would run off, and the first grill that cooked food from both the top and the bottom, it had some unique selling points.

So the grill was being marketed from a health perspective, not simply as another grill in the marketplace. That's how it was differenti-ated. Rick believed that this point of difference, along with a celebrity like George lending his force to the marketing, would translate to sales success.

Well, that didn't happen. The infomercial aired for several months, at a cost of several hundred thousand dollars, and its message failed to connect.

A little more due diligence was done. Research revealed that over 80 percent of the people watching the infomercial and likely to make the purchasing decision on an item like this were female. The lesson:

Know your customer. Females aren't generally huge boxing fans. So they took George Foreman out of the boxing ring and put him in a kitchen. They took off his heavyweight belt and swapped it for an apron. They reshot the infomercial using a female host and went back on the air. Within 12 months, the George Foreman Grill was doing several hundred million dollars in revenue.

Today, nine out of ten people I talk to own either one or multiple George Foreman Grills. The marketing and the product created a WOW experience. They connected with their customer with a health message. They created their own playing field and dominated it.

The company that was responsible for the George Foreman Grill bought out George Foreman's endorsement contract for the product. The price tag for that was over $126 million in cash and stock. At the time, it was bigger than the deal Nike made with Michael Jordan. It was the biggest single product endorsement in history, a pretty amazing fact that few people know.

CUMBERLAND DIAMOND EXCHANGE

I worked with a local business here in Atlanta called Cumberland Diamond Exchange. Mark Jacobson, his wife Rhonda, and his brother Wayne exemplify going the extra mile for customers. They make you feel like family the moment you walk into their store. They are truly creating a WOW experience by treating you like royalty when you walk through the door. You are greeted with a warm smile, offered a beverage and then serviced by the most knowledgeable staff in the industry. They don't try to sell you; they educate you so you can make an informed decision.

And as a result, their business has been thriving for over 20 years. When others are struggling in this down economy, they are receiving national recognition for their outstanding service and knowledge in their industry.

Why? The Jacobson's are not in the jewelry business. They are in the people-pleasing business, and it makes all the difference. They create a WOW experience because they're passionate about what they do. They do it better than anybody else.

DR. HATRAK

I work with a chiropractor here in Atlanta named Dr. Michael Hatrak. There are about 40,000 working chiropractors in Atlanta, so the first thing we did when we started working together, was rebrand Dr. Hatrak. Instead of competing against 40,000 chiropractors, we positioned Dr. Hatrak as a certified Synergy Release Physician. He developed an entire certification program for candidates wishing to become a certified Synergy Release Physician, and now trains other chiropractors to be certified.

I've worked with Dr. Hatrak and his team on creating a WOW experience for his clients, and they have grown and moved from a 1,900-square-foot nondescript office building behind a fast-food restaurant into a 5,000-square-foot Class-A, state-of-the-art office space, which they transformed into a state-of-the-art clinical environment.

Dr. Hatrak works with over 450 pro athletes, and this is part of the WOW experience he creates for his clients. When you go to his facility, you feel like you are being given the same caliber of treatment professional athletes receive. As a matter of fact, when you walk into his office, chances are good that you'll rub elbows with a professional athlete.

THE REWARDS OF CREATING A WOW EXPERIENCE IN YOUR PERSONAL LIFE

By now, you clearly see the value and benefit of creating a WOW experience at the business level. But what about creating it in your personal life?

Recently, a man I know was talking about a deal he was trying to put together with "his biggest client." Another young man, an attorney, told him, "Your wife and your family are your biggest client." It's true. Your spouse and your family are your biggest single client, collectively, and they deserve WOW experiences.

So how can you create a WOW experience at home? How can you create a WOW experience in your marriage? How can you create a WOW experience in your relationship with your children? The same principles and concepts that apply for business apply here. You need to do more than exceed expectations. You need to amaze them.

To me, it is unacceptable to be a success in business and a failure at home. And by applying these same principles, by rejecting passivity and being intentional, by taking responsibility and looking for ways to constantly create a WOW experience, you can improve the quality of your relationships.

A MISSION STATEMENT FOR MARRIAGE

My wife and I developed a mission statement for our marriage and for our family, along with a set of values for which our family stands. Some people might think this is going to an unnecessary extreme—but if it's so important to have a mission and a vision for your business, shouldn't you have a mission and a vision for your marriage and your family?

Here's the mission statement that Indy and I agreed on for our marriage:

> *The mission of our marriage is to love each other unconditionally and to continually encourage and support each other in all areas of life. We are lifelong partners committed forever to bring out the best in each other as we strive to reach our full potential.*

How can you create a WOW experience in your marriage, or your relationship? You know best what your partner likes (and *really* likes), so I'll leave the nitty-gritty particulars up to you. But following are some guidelines that will help. I often work with couples to help them establish goals for their marriage, and these five areas of focus can help stimulate ideas. My wife and I are also currently working on a marriage book.

To have a WOW experience in your marriage, you need to have:

1. Purposeful communication

One of the greatest lessons I have learned is that my wife doesn't want me to fix her problems. Most of the time, she just wants to know that I am listening to her and that I hear her. So now I always ask the question, do you want me to respond or do you want me to listen? Another great tool is one I call *React and Reject vs. Reflect and Respond.* When you are in a conversation, it is always better to take time and understand what the other person is saying rather than automatically reject what they have to say.

How could you make the communication with your partner more purposeful and empathetic?

2. Perseverance

After you get married you have two jobs to do: *You must be be committed to keeping the marriage going, and you must be committed to making the marriage great.* As with anything else in life, you have to keep learning and growing in a marriage or you will become stagnant. When you are better educated about the realities of marriage, you have a bigger toolbox, and you are better equipped to build a higher-quality relationship. There's an enormous supply of resources covering virtually every aspect of marriage. You name it, from communication and conflict resolution to intimacy, there's a virtual ocean of learning possibilities.

What are you reading, watching and listening to that's helping you move your relationship in the direction that you want to go?

3. Intentional, consistent actions

Just as with exercise, small deposits made on a consistent basis will keep your relationship fresh and exciting. Having goals for your marriage will help in this area. Schedule date nights together, plan vacations and surprise each other with kind acts or gifts that are not for any specific occasion. Get creative when it comes to your marriage and good things will follow.

In what ways could you grow closer by traveling the extra mile for your spouse on a consistent basis? In what ways could you really surprise your spouse in the next 12 months or in the next 30 days? What type of surprises would you like your spouse to be planning for you?

4. Clear priorities

My wife, Indy, always reminds me that we have to deal with the *whole pie*. We have the social, emotional, spiritual, financial, intellectual and physical aspects of our marriage, and we must always try to keep them in harmony. It is a balancing act. If you take care of several pieces of the pie, but ignore one that needs attention, it can have a major impact on you and your marriage.

What piece of the pie do you need to work on the most?

5. Progress, not perfection

There are no perfect people, so there are no perfect relationships. As I mentioned before, it's easy in any relationship to find someone doing something wrong and scold them for it, but it works much better if you can find your spouse doing something right and praise him or her for it.

What can you praise your partner for today? Remember, you are not looking for anything in return. You will be amazed at what can happen to a relationship if one or both people do this.

"Treat a man as he is, he will remain so. Treat a man the way he can be and ought to be, and he will become as he can be and should be."

JOHANN WOLFGANG VON GOETHE

INDY'S BIRTHDAY PARTY

Here's a specific example of something I did to go the extra mile for my wife. It was her 40th birthday, and I had planned a small dinner with some friends and family at a restaurant she really enjoys in Atlanta. As we were sitting there eating, what my wife didn't know, was that I had invited the rest of the family and about 100 of her friends, many of whom she hadn't seen since high school. People came from all over the country.

They were all waiting upstairs in a separate room in the restaurant. When we finished eating our dinner, I said, "We're going to have dessert upstairs in a special place." As we walked into the room to a warm ovation, Indy was naturally shocked.

It took a lot of time, planning and effort, but it was certainly worth it.

That's just one example. But when you go the extra mile, it doesn't have to be extravagant or expensive. Any small act can let your partner know that you're thinking about them.

"THIS MONTH, I TRAVEL THE EXTRA MILE FOR…"

Here's an exercise that we use when we conduct couples retreats. We have our couples fill out little cards that have "This month I travel the extra mile for_____ by _____" written on them. For example, I would write "Indy," my wife, or the name of one of my children (or anyone in my life) in the first blank space. In the second blank, I would write the action I want to take to go the extra mile for that person. We collect these at the end of the conference, and then each month we send them back to each partner as reminders of what they wanted to do.

It's a great exercise to keep your spouse and your children on the top of your mind and to create those moments that can impact them so positively.

CHAPTER 9:

GET MORE HPA IN YOUR DAY

"Lost time is never found again."

BENJAMIN FRANKLIN

In 2008, I was giving a keynote talk in Chicago to a group of over 400 actuaries.

They say that the definition of an actuary is "an accountant without a personality" (no offense intended to actuaries), but I really wanted to connect with this group.

At the start of the talk, I showed a slide with a big red number— 525,600. I've mentioned this number in an earlier chapter so it may be familiar to you.

"Does anybody know what this number represents?" I asked.

There were various answers, and after a few minutes someone correctly said that it was the number of minutes in every year. I told them my task in this presentation was to help them maximize every one of those minutes in order to get the most out of business and out of life.

As I was talking, I noticed a hand waving wildly near the front of the room. Again, as this was a keynote talk, it really wasn't meant to be an interactive presentation. I asked the young lady, "Can I help you?" She told me that there would not be 525,600 minutes in 2008. It was a leap year, so there are 527,040 minutes. "That's why you're an actuary," I told her.

Well, whether there are 525,600 or 527,040 minutes in a given year, we all have the same amount of time, but we don't all use it the same way. We have already talked about taking action. Now we're going to talk about taking the *right actions* and making the most out of every minute we have.

The Dash
By Linda Ellis

I read of a man who stood to speak at a funeral of a friend.

He referred to the dates on her tombstone from the beginning to the end.

He noted that first came the date of her birth and spoke of the following date with tears.

But he said what mattered most of all was the dash between those years.

For that dash represents all the time that she spent alive on earth,

and now only those who love her know what that little line is worth.

For it matters not how much we own, the cars, the house, the cash.

What matters is how we live and love and how we spend our dash.
So think about this long and hard.

Are there things you'd like to change?

For you never know how much time is left that can still be rearranged.

If we could just slow down enough to consider what's true and real

and always try to understand the way other people feel,

and be less quick to anger and show appreciation more,

and love the people in our lives like we've never loved before.

If we treat each other with respect and more often wear a smile,

remembering that this special dance might only last a little while.
So when your eulogy is being read with your life's actions to rehash,

would you be proud of the things they say about how you spent your dash?

I love this poem. Linda Ellis was a virtually unknown poet until this poem was read on the radio one day. The phone lines lit up at the radio station. Since then, it has changed her life, and she's gone on to become a nationally acclaimed poet. Millions of people have read "The Dash" and responded to the reality of it.

How will you "live your dash?" As you know, a three-page letter from one of my father's friends written way back in 1968 told me how my dad lived his dash, and helped me define how I live mine.

One way I want to live my dash is to practice something that I've learned. I've learned that is not the things we accumulate in life or how long we live that determines our success, but rather the hearts we touch along the way and the difference we make in the lives of others.

That's really what the dash is all about.

When all is said and done, the significance of our lives—the dash—will be a reflection of the choices we make. And since we only go around once in life, we need to choose wisely.

THE PARADOX OF TIME

There is always enough time to achieve what needs to be accomplished. But there is never enough time to do everything.

This means that the key to successful living lies in taking action on your most important priorities and continually simplifying your life by removing the junk from it.

There is always enough time to do the *right* things. Determining what those right things are can be challenging, especially when we are constantly bombarded by so many distractions, cultural trends and suggestions. The clamor and noise in life can distract even the most focused person.

No matter who you are or what you do, your progress and success in life will depend, more than any other factor, on how you choose to invest the 24 hours, the 1,440 minutes, the 86,400 seconds that you are given each day.

SURFING THE INTERNET: A MONSTER TIME-WASTER

I read an interesting statistic. It stated that people who use the Internet spend an average of 60 hours per month online: 22 percent spend it on social networking, 41 percent spend it on viewing content, and 36 percent spend it on email or surfing the net.

BUT IT'S JUST 15 MINUTES...

Think of this. Misusing just 15 minutes a day, over the course of a year, can cost you 90 hours. That's more than two full work weeks.

Are the *years* you may spend online really worthy of your dash?

For many people, the endless hours on the Internet are a massive time-waster, and a low-payback activity. Cut back, and spend more time on more rewarding activities and pursuits.

TOPS

I was blessed to be the chairman of an organization called TOPS. This is an acronym for the Techwood Outreach Program through Sports. It was started by Bill Maness, a graduate of Furman. Right in the shadows of Georgia Tech was one of the worst housing projects in Atlanta—and in the country.

In that housing project, the statistics were harsh: Only 1 out of 126 children would graduate from college.

I remember going to those housing projects for the first time. It was scary. They were infested with violence and drugs. The data showed that a lot of children came from single-parent homes. The boys and young men, in particular, did not have a successful male role model to show them how to live life. So they would resort to violence and other negative acts.

I spoke to a group of children from these housing projects while working with TOPS, and asked them, "What's your goal? What's your dream?"

One specific response stood out. A boy who was 12 years old said he wanted to get a girl pregnant before he turned 15, because he wouldn't live to be 16. In his perspective, his dash wasn't going to represent very much, and there wasn't much to live for. So he had a very short-term focus. That young man accomplished his goal when he was 13 years old. He became a dad.

We found, over time, that throwing money at the social problems in these housing projects yielded very little benefit. Creating great programs didn't help much, either. What made the most difference was having a consistent presence in the life of these young men who were not used to having a male role model. The best investment we made was investing our time and energy to establish trust with these young men.

We did this for six years. The first two young men who had gone through the program continued to excel and overcome the challenges of their environment as they grew. Those two young men were exposed not only to sports but to the experience of working in successful businesses.

I'll never forget the day I drove those two young men to college. They were given a vision of what is possible in life beyond the environment that they were brought up in, and they expanded their dash.

It wasn't giving them a handout. It was giving them a hand up. And it created a longer-term focus. Several years later, the former mayor of Atlanta, Andrew Young, wrote that TOPS was one of the best programs of its type and should be used on a national level to help lift people up.

To me, it's amazing what people can accomplish in every aspect of their life when they can identify ways to expand their dash. And the outcomes or results usually come from the choices they make. You and I have the ability, every day, to choose what it is we focus our attention, effort and energy on. And I've learned that the most successful people in life—the clients I work with that grow the quickest in their business and their personal relationships—are the ones that choose wisely. They are the ones who focus on what I call *high-payback activities* in each area of their life.

One of the biggest breakthroughs occurs when clients identify their high-payback activities, or HPAs, and find ways to spend more time working on them. Usually their high-payback activities will also line up with their genius, which we discussed in chapter four. Remember, your genius is what you're most passionate about and also what you're really good at doing.

When my clients identify their high-payback activities and spend more time engaged in them—and delegate or get rid of their *low-payback activities*—they make the biggest breakthroughs. This is where you will make the biggest breakthrough too, because then you won't just be taking action, but you'll be taking the *right* actions that move you closer to becoming the person you want to be.

HIGH-PAYBACK ACTIVITIES

Below are my definitions of a high-payback activity.

On a business level: The actions or activities that create the results for which you get compensated, or that create the results that move you closer to the mission of the company.

On a personal level: The actions or activities that create the results that move you closer to becoming the person you're striving to become, and help to lift up the people in your circle of influence.

Here is my definition of a low-payback activity: Anything you can delegate or get rid of that does not add value on a business or personal level.

It's pretty simple. After you have defined your goals, and developed a compelling reason *why* you want to accomplish these goals, the next step is to identify the top three to five high-payback activities in each area that will help you accomplish them.

YOU ARE ONLY REALLY WORKING WHEN YOU ARE WORKING ON YOUR HIGH-PAYBACK ACTIVITIES

Let me show you my own high-payback activities, which I've identified in five key areas of my life.

The first key area is **marriage**, though for you it may be another relationship. My top high-payback activity in my marriage is **spending quality time with my wife**, Indy. In a book I highly recommend, *The Five Love Languages*, Gary Chapman identifies quality time as one of the specific things people tend to crave most. (I tend to crave words of affirmation, by the way, because I didn't receive a lot of words of affirmation when I was growing up.) Typically, in our relationship, we tend to give the other person what we crave ourselves. If you want to know what your partner craves, just ask.

Praying together is another high-payback activity for my wife and me. It didn't come very naturally to me at first, but I persevered. One study showed that out of 1,700 couples that were followed over a ten-year period, the couples that stayed together often prayed together. In fact, the divorce rate for couples that pray together is less than one percent. Basically, that says to me that "the couples that pray together stay together." So we have made praying together one of the high-payback activities in our marriage. We have found it is difficult to be mad at someone you pray with.

In **business**, one of my high-payback activities is speaking. When I am speaking to people, I am in my genius. I am working on what I'm passionate about and what I do very well. When I am speaking to people, it's also a natural networking environment because people want to ask questions. They want to learn more about the things I talk about, which leads to consulting opportunities that help grow my business.

Another high-payback activity for me is developing content and products. I'm constantly looking at how to take my information and develop it into content that will be relevant to the people that need it, to help them get unstuck. It's a goal of mine to help them move their life in a direction that will improve their business and improve their personal lives.

The third focus area for me is **health and fitness**. One of my high-payback activities in this arena is eating five to six nutritional meals and snacks per day instead of three big heavy meals. I am very aware of what I put into my body. I'm 56 years old. I'm 6'2". I weigh about 205 pounds. When my body fat is low, I feel really good.

Sleeping is another a high-payback activity in my health area, even though it doesn't sound like an activity. If I don't get six to eight hours of sleep, then I'm not as effective as I could be mentally and physically.

Running and cycling are HPAs, as well. I do one or the other five days a week. I try to cycle once or twice a week, and then run three to four times a week. For me, those are high-payback activities.

The fourth area is **spiritual**. An HPA here involves reading a daily devotional or doing a Bible study. While praying together is a marriage HPA, I also try to pray on my own every day.

In every area, when I do my HPAs, I have more energy. I am more in tune and in sync with my life. I am more productive in my business. Conversely, if I remove any of the high-payback activities in any of those areas, my quality of life starts going downhill.

AN HPA EXERCISE

Here's a high-payback activity exercise that you will find quite easy to do. It will help you identify the HPAs that most effectively move you in the direction you need to go.

Identify your different key areas of life and write them down. They will likely be **business, personal, health and fitness, marriage** or **relationship, parenting** (if appropriate) and **spiritual**. Feel free to add your own areas. You can also add a financial area if you wish.

For every area of life, write three high-payback activities that you have identified. What are the three steps or acts that would yield the greatest return in each area?

Remember, these are the actions, activities or choices that create results that will help you become the person you want to become, or help generate compensation.

The top three in each area should be obvious to you; they are probably the frogs (remember chapter five?) that you've been doing everything you can to avoid eating. Take the time to do this exercise, because if you don't know what your high-payback activities are in each key area of life, you will be lost.

LOW-PAYBACK ACTIVITIES

As important as the high-payback activities are, some of the biggest transformations my clients experience, have come from identifying the opposite. They identified their low-payback activities, or LPAs.

As I've already mentioned, these are the activities you need to delegate or eliminate.

If you work for somebody else, this can be a little tricky because you must adhere to their agenda and sometimes engage in low-payback activities. But in my experience, I have found that the people who excel in organizations are the ones who can focus more on the HPAs and delegate or get rid of the LPAs. Even with the most unreasonable of bosses, it can still be done.

What are some examples of LPAs?

1. Doing things other people want you to do.

This is their agenda versus your agenda. Meetings are big culprits. Whenever I call a meeting, I always state the goal of the meeting. I often ask this when I attend meetings. I ask that people prepare the goal in advance. Then I always ask the bigger question: Is the meeting really necessary?

Meetings need to have a goal. You need to have agenda. You need to be prepared and, before scheduling one at all, ask the really important question: Is the meeting necessary?

2. Doing things a certain way because "this is the way we've always done it."

In my consulting work, I've found that this causes more LPAs than anything else. Due to traditions or habits, people get used to doing things a certain way. In any organization, people tend to take on the culture of that company. Remember, we tend to take on the habits of the people we spend the most time with. These people may say, *"We've always done it this way. Why should we change now?"*

Well, here's one of the rules that I've implemented in every company I've had: When it comes to productivity and the way we do things to create results, if you have a more effective way of doing any of them, *speak up*. We give people incentives to do this. We make a point of rewarding people who have saved the company money by doing something differently, or revealing an opportunity for a new revenue stream. We compensate them and give them a percentage of the new business.

3. Doing things you are not good at doing.

I know what my strengths are. I'm what they call a "rainmaker." I have a great ability to influence people. I'm very good at identifying problems. I can see problems from a gut, instinctual level.

But I'm not the classic "detail person."

For example, I am not good at developing graphics for presentations. I delegate that responsibility to the other people on my team who are extremely good at this. They can create a WOW experience through graphics. I can't. More accurately, any WOW that someone may utter in response to seeing a graphic I created certainly wouldn't be positive.

4. Doing things you don't enjoy doing.

When you don't enjoy doing something, you won't have your heart in it and you won't do it well. Of course, there will always be things in your work or personal life you don't enjoy doing. But the more you can decrease them, and the more you can work in your genius, the more productive you're going to be.

When you identify specific tasks that you're not good at doing or that you don't enjoy doing, realize that there is almost assuredly someone in your organization who loves to do them—and is very good at doing them. We're all wired differently, and we all have different interests and different abilities. Your LPA is someone else's HPA.

The secret on any team is finding those people, and delegating those LPAs that you don't like doing or don't do well. Again, the more you can make this happen, the more successful you're going to be.

HOW MUCH IS YOUR TIME WORTH?

Here's a great exercise I do with my clients: I have them determine the value of their time. Consider that if you make $50,000 per year and you work 40 hours a week, you average about $26.04 an hour. If you make $50,000 and work 60 hours a week, you make $17.36 an hour. The math here isn't difficult. Just divide your annual salary by the number of hours you work every year.

If you work...	That adds up to...
20 hours a week	960 hours per year
30 hours a week	1,440 hours per year
40 hours a week,	1,920 hours per year
50 hours a week	2,400 hours per year
60 hours a week	2,880 hours per year

Take your annual salary and divide it by the number of hours worked in a year, and you will come up with your hourly rate. This was an eye-opening exercise for me. It gave me a benchmark to make decisions.

If you're asked to do something that will generate much less than your typical hourly rate, try to delegate it. One of my employees was making about $125,000 a year and working about 50 hours a week. That comes out to $52.08 per hour. I had been recommending for years that he hire an assistant. Why? He was mired in low-payback activities; a lot of administrative stuff, scheduling, emails.

I said, "You need to hire an assistant and pay them $40,000 a year out of your own pocket."

He resisted for almost a year, but finally relented. Within 12 months, he was making $225,000 per year.

Now, was that investment of delegating his low-payback activities to his assistant worth the $40,000 a year he paid out? It absolutely was.

Once you have this perspective on how you spend your time and how much your time is worth, you have a benchmark to determine if you are doing a low-payback activity or not. If you make $150,000 a year working 50 hours a week, your rate is $62.50 per hour. If you find yourself doing work you could pay someone $12 an hour to do so you can continue to focus on your high-payback activities that would obviously be worth it.

Now, you may not be in a position to hire an assistant, but *I guarantee you are in a position to get rid of some of your low payback activities.*

Your time is valuable. The more you understand the value of your time, the more you will understand how important it is to guard it and use it wisely, focusing on HPAs in your business and relationships.

CHAPTER 10:

UNDERSTAND THE IMPORTANCE OF BALANCE

"We come into this world head first and go out feet first; in between, it is all a matter of balance."

PAUL BOESE

A vacationing American businessman stood on the pier of a quaint coastal fishing village in southern Mexico. He watched as a small boat with a single young Mexican fisherman aboard pulled into the dock. Inside the small boat were several large yellow fin tuna. Enjoying the warmth of the early afternoon sun, the American complimented the Mexican on the quality of his fish.

"How long did it take you to catch them?" the American casually asked.

"Oh, a few hours," the Mexican fisherman replied.

"Why don't you stay out longer and catch more fish?" the American businessman then asked.

The Mexican warmly replied, "With this, I have more than enough to support my family's needs."

The businessman then became serious. "But what do you do with the rest of your time?"

Responding with a smile, the Mexican fisherman answered, "I sleep late, play with my children, watch ball games and take siestas with my wife. Sometimes in the evenings I take a stroll into the village to see my friends, play the guitar and sing a few songs."

The American businessman impatiently interrupted. "Look, I have an MBA from Harvard, and I can help you to be more profitable. You can start by fishing several hours longer every day. You can then sell the extra fish you catch. With the extra money you can buy a bigger boat. With the additional income that larger boat will bring, before long, you can buy a second boat and a third one and so on until you have an entire fleet of fishing boats."

Proud of his own sharp thinking, he excitedly elaborated a grand scheme which could bring even bigger profits. "Then, instead of selling your catch to a middleman, you'll be able to sell your fish directly to the processor or even open your own cannery. Eventually you could control the product, processing and distribution. You could leave this tiny coastal village and move to Mexico City or possibly even Los Angeles or New York City where you could expand your enterprise even more."

Having never thought of such things, the Mexican fisherman asked, "But how long will all this take?"

After a rapid mental calculation, the Harvard MBA pronounced, "Probably about 15 to 20 years, maybe less if you work really hard."

"And then what, señor?" asked the fisherman.

"Why, that's the best part," answered the businessman, with a laugh. "When the time is right, you would sell your company stock to the public and become very rich. You would make millions."

"Millions? Really? What would I do with it all?" asked the young fisherman in disbelief.

The businessman boasted, "Then you could happily retire with all the money you've made. You could move to a quaint coastal fishing village where you could sleep late, play with your grandchildren, watch ball games and take siestas with your wife. You could stroll to the village in the evenings where you could play the guitar and sing with your friends all you want."

"But señor, I already do that," the young fisherman replied.

"The price of anything is the amount of life you have to exchange for it."

HENRY DAVID THOREAU

Over the years, I have worked with thousands of people through my seminars, consulting and speaking. And whenever I ask the question, "What is your greatest challenge in life?" nine times out of ten, **it is balancing work with family or home life**. I believe this is even more prevalent today. With the down economy, statistics show that more than 50 percent of families are dual-income earners. And it makes that balancing act even more difficult.

I have found that one of the biggest reasons for lack of balance is simply that people are not intentional about their choices and priorities, so they tend to let life happen to them instead of taking the time to create clarity, develop a plan and take action to implement it.

THE CARDINAL

My wife and I used to live in an area where a beautiful red cardinal lived. Cardinals are very territorial birds and will fight off intruding birds aggressively. We had just purchased a new car, and I remember coming out in the morning to see the cardinal attacking the mirror, constantly flying away and then flying back into the mirror.

What a stupid bird, I thought to myself. His enemy is merely a reflection of himself in the mirror. And then it came to me. You know, we can be our own worst enemy and not realize it. By the choices we make, by the people we associate with, by the habits we practice, we tend to live our life as it happens rather than being intentional on how we want to live life, and that is how we get out of balance. It's not on purpose. It's usually by default. The only way to get into balance is to make it a priority, develop a plan—and develop specific action steps to make it happen.

What is important to you? Is it your leisure time, career, friends, family, volunteer work, your faith, hobbies or sports? Because we all have different priorities, goals and values, there is no one-size-fits all to achieving a balanced life.

THE BALANCE TEST

Let me give you a quick test to see if your life is in balance. I want you to answer these questions, true or false.

1. I live a healthy lifestyle that helps me feel energized.

2. I have sufficient time to do what I enjoy doing.

3. I am passionate about my work, and find it satisfying and rewarding.

4. I love the environment I live in (contents and location).

5. I have quantity and quality time for my family or important relationships.

6. I eat healthy, nutritious foods that make me feel energized.

7. I take at least 15 minutes of quiet time each day.

8. I have clarity on my passion and purpose in life.

9. I have friends who encourage and support me and whose company I enjoy.

10. I get six to eight hours of sleep each day.

11. I have no emotional baggage or addictive behaviors.

12. I focus on my blessings and not my problems.

13. I have activities or hobbies outside of work and family.

14. I do not work on weekends.

15. I am organized and have no clutter in my home, car or office.

16. I am excited when I wake up to take on the day.

17. I take at least two weeks of vacation per year.

18. I do not have any people in my life who drain me.

19. I feel like I am in control of my schedule and my time.

20. I am pursuing what I want in life.

21. I love my life.

So, how did you do? Typically, if you answered 15 or more of these questions true, that indicates you have a reasonably balanced life. If you answered 14 or fewer of these questions true, you have room to improve the balance in your life. The fewer questions you answered true, the more room for improvement you have.

Don't get me wrong; there will always be times when certain aspects of your life are out of balance. I remember several years ago when my wife Indy was working on her doctorate. Our lives were basically turned upside down. She was out of balance, and our lives were out of balance because she had to focus so much time, effort and energy on studying and going to class.

So there are always going to be difficult times. But here's what I want you to remember about balance: It's all about progress, not perfection. It's about moving from where you are currently and becoming more intentional about creating balance in your life.

THE CESARI FAMILY VALUES

As I've mentioned quite a bit in this book, my wife Indy and I have four children. When they were younger, we developed what we called the *Cesari Family Values*. We developed these with our children and we posted them on our refrigerator. To this day, I still carry a small wallet-sized version with me. Your own family values will depend on several factors, including the environment you were brought up in and your own particular beliefs. Here are the values we developed for our family.

1. **Let your actions speak for your beliefs. Be sure anything you're doing will glorify God.**

2. **Respect one another. Be loyal, encouraging, kind, uplifting and positive.**

3. **Always strive to be honest and truthful in all situations.**

4. **Forgive others, even when you feel they don't deserve it.** It's easy to love people who are loveable. The real trick in life is to love those who aren't very loveable, and forgiveness works the same way.

5. **Practice unconditional love.** We would always tell our children, "Look, we might not always like or agree with what you are doing, but there is nothing you could ever do that will ever make us stop loving you."

6. **Stand by each others' side at all times and in all situations.**

7. **Be humble and God-centered, not self-centered.**

8. **Seek to understand the other person before you seek to be understood.**

Now, again, don't get me wrong. We're not the perfect family, but we do know what we stand for. And what I have found is, if you don't know what you stand for, you will fall for anything. Once you have taken time to identify your core values, you are then ready for the next steps.

A PARENTING MISSION STATEMENT

Indy and I developed a goal for our parenting:

To model and mentor for our children and their children a life dedicated to loving God and loving each other unconditionally.

EIGHT PRINCIPLES TO ADD BALANCE

How can we begin to bring balance to our lives? I've developed eight concepts and principles that I have taught over the years. I've learned from other people and my own experiences that these are the best ways to bring balance to your life.

1. Clarify and prioritize your values.

A value is defined as *a principle standard of quality, considered worthwhile or desired.* Values guide our actions, and they are usually a result of our life experiences. When you are clear on your core values, it helps to determine the choices you make and what you say yes to and what you say no to.

Policies are many, principles are few. Policies always change; principles never do. Principles and values become the foundation by which you filter all of the other things that you potentially do in life. Your values become the guidelines that help you make decisions. I have found that people who lack good, strong core values tend to wander through life more than the people who have good, clear values and make their decisions based on them.

A litmus test for every decision: Given the values that I stand for, will this action or choice (or relationship, or opportunity, etc.) help move me closer to the person I want to become, or will it move me farther away?

2. Make sure your goals are in harmony with your core values.

If they are not, it can create tension and stress in your life. We've already touched on this in the book, but it's an extremely important part of developing balance and it bears repeating.

Let me give you an example. If it's important for you to have dinner with your family but it's also important for you to work late, it will create stress. It will create dissonance. The whole idea behind balance is to have less stress and more time to do the things that are important to you. Being intentional and setting goals that are *in line with your core values* will help you reduce stress and stay focused on those things that are really important to you.

3. Manage your time.

Or someone else will. When you don't have clarity on what your purpose is or what your goals are, you will tend to let everyone and anyone take up your time. And that's a recipe for imbalance.

When I ask my clients what their priorities are in life, it usually goes something like this: Faith or God, family or spouse, and then work.

My next question is the eye-opener. I ask, "Well, how much time do you actually spend in each of those areas on a given day?"

Now, I know we have an obligation to work a certain amount of hours. That's reality. But are you really managing your time based on your most important priorities in life?

I've personally found that the biggest regret most people have is that they didn't spend enough **time** with those who meant the most to them: Their wife or husband, their children, or other family members. Many people who have been extremely successful from a worldly perspective leave a trail of broken relationships behind them. To be truly successful, you must make certain that you're devoting time to the people and things that are most important to you.

In order to do that, you're frequently going to be forced to say no to some very good opportunities. I used to say yes to everybody who asked me for my time. Yes, I will meet you. Yes, I will go to that event. Yes, I will participate in that fundraiser. Yes, I will be happy to meet with your son or your daughter. I felt like I was supposed to give my time to anybody who asked. I thought that I was being polite.

But I found that as I started saying no, it gave me the opportunity to say yes to the right things—the things that were congruent with my values, and my passion and purpose in life.

STEFAN

My friend Stefan is 37 years old. He works four and a half days a week in the financial service industry and he is usually finished with work by 3 p.m. He works hard and he earns a great living. He plays hard, and he spends lots of time with his family.

How much time?

He takes ten weeks of vacation a year.

Ten weeks.

That's two and a half months, or almost 25 percent of the year.

You may be saying, "Well, Steve, that sounds great. Stefan owns his own company."

He doesn't. Stefan works for a company. He came up

WHAT'S MOST IMPORTANT TO YOU? IN WHAT ORDER?

Sit down and rank the things that are most important to you, whatever they are. In my life, the ranking goes like this: God, my wife, my children, then my business and then exercising. So I try to schedule my time around all of those things, and I am intentional about putting those things on my calendar and my organizer.

Right now, take the time to help balance your life by scheduling time to do those things that are most important to you. Schedule a date night once a week with your spouse. Schedule a time to write a letter or call a friend. Schedule time to take a trip with your family.

with a formula that allows him to work very hard, creating the results he needs to create for his employer, and then spend the extra time with his family. He presented the plan to his boss and convinced his boss to give it a try.

Stefan is a devoted dad and devoted husband. He could work longer hours and make a lot more money. But he has clear priorities and goals. To him, it's more important to spend time with his family, to take vacations, than it is to make more money.

As Stefan says, "I work harder than anyone else when I am at work, and I give honest, sincere appreciation to those who deserve it, beginning with my family."

4. Maintain a high-energy lifestyle.

I spoke in detail about this in chapter one, but it's a critical part of living in balance. Having a high-energy lifestyle is really the key to being able to do everything else you want to accomplish. If you're run down, or sick, you can't hope to have a balanced life.

5. Don't *should* on yourself.

If you are like me, you sometimes look back on life and say to yourself, "I should have done this, I should have done that." Cut yourself some slack. One of the worst things you can do is to go through life feeling guilty. You need to understand your limitations and be realistic.

I have come to realize that I am not perfect, and there are no perfect people. So I don't expect perfect outcomes for everything I do. Remember, we are looking for progress, not perfection. I used to spend a lot of time comparing myself to other people. If only I had *his* job. If only I came from *his* family. If only, if only, if only.

When I stopped comparing myself to everyone else and began to build confidence in myself and my abilities, I didn't have the time or desire to compare myself anymore.

Don't compare yourself to anyone else because *there is no one else like you.*

When I'm at my seminars, I will sometimes ask everyone to look at their hand and specifically at their fingers. I then remind them that there is no one else in this world that has the same fingerprints as them. They are unique, one of a kind. And each one of them has unique gifts and talents that will impact the world in a way that only they can.

There is no other you, so cut yourself some slack. Stop *shoulding* on yourself and start living the life that *only you can live.*

6. Live in the present.

There's a great book entitled *The Present* by Spencer Johnson, M.D. that gives these three tips:

1. Be in the present. When you want to be happier and more successful, focus on what is right now. Respond to what is important now.

2. Learn from the past. When you want to make the present better than the past, look at what happened in the past. Learn something valuable from it. Do things differently in the present.

3. Plan for the future. When you want to make the future better for the present, see what a wonderful future would look like. Make plans to help it happen and then put your plan into action in the present.

Stay in the moment. Today is the only thing that we have to work with. Tomorrow is not guaranteed. Yesterday is gone. So stay with the present and deal with what's important now.

7. Turn off the TV.

Or at least turn it on a little less often. This is probably going to be one of the toughest ones to tackle.

I like television. I have certain shows that I watch faithfully. But it's selective watching. And as I've mentioned, my wife and I were very intentional with our children when it came to the TV. We required that they did an hour of reading before they could watch a half hour of TV.

HAVE A BLACKBERRY?

I do. I typically turn my Black-Berry off at 6:00 p.m. unless I have pre-arranged a phone call. That's when it's time to be with my family. I turn it off so I don't see the red email blinking telling me that I have a text and or an email. *I turn it off.* Have I missed many "emergencies?" No. If people need to reach me after hours, they can call me on my home phone number—and I find many people are more reluctant to do that then they are to just speed dial you on their cell at 8 p.m. So there are far fewer emergencies.

Why? It's all too easy to overdose on TV. In fact, in a three-month period in 2010, Nielsen reported that the average American television viewer watched more than 151 hours of television per month, an all-time high, up from more than 145 hours during the same period in 2009.

This doesn't count the additional screen time on computers and other handheld devices. Nielsen also found that Americans are watching more videos on their cell phones.

If you just turn off the television, you will gain five hours per day. What could you do with those five hours?

If you just cut down by half the amount of TV that the average family watches, that will give you two and a half hours a day. Two and a half hours to interact with your loved ones. Two and a half hours to give back to your community. Two and a half hours to exercise. Two and a half hours to read a book.

8. Be creative.

"Think outside the box," as the cliché goes. Think outside the box in your work and also in your personal life. Nothing takes the excitement out of life as much as getting stuck in the same routine. Do something out of the ordinary to avoid the well-worn routines of your life. Try a new route to work, a new radio station. Break out of your mold occasionally. If you're a runner, try something different. Try cycling. Try swimming. Try anything different.

If your spouse usually plans dates and vacations, shake it up and do this yourself and try something new. Read a good book on intimacy. Travel someplace you've never traveled before. Try painting or writing or photography. Meet new people. It's important to socialize. Your employer expects you to be vibrant and enthusiastic and healthy. Your friends want you to go to ball games and block parties and volunteer to build a habitat house.

To keep your life balanced you need to meet new people and exercise your wit, your wisdom, your humor and your charm. They say the only difference between who you are today and who you will be five years from now will come from the people you meet and the books you read. Are you choosing both with any sense of purpose? Spend time around other people who can help you think of new, creative ways to put spice in your life and to put some pep in your step and to help you be more energized at work, at home and in the community. You can do it. You have the ability. You just have to be intentional about it.

Be creative at work. There are so many people who operate a virtual corporation right now. In fact, part of my company is virtual. I have some of the best people in the country working for me, but they're not on my payroll. They just work with me on specific projects. I spend about 25 percent of my time speaking, 50 percent consulting and the other 25 percent developing products. Most of the consulting is done by my virtual staff.

I have one independent contractor in particular who has a demanding personal life. She's married. She has young children. And she can only work between the hours of 9:00 a.m. and 1:00 p.m. But you know what? We got creative, and she got creative. We work around her family schedule and allow her the flexibility to work from home when it is convenient for her. And she is one of the best associates I have ever worked with. She's very good at what she does—and this is one huge reason why I took efforts to allow the arrangement to work. She works about 15 hours a week, and our clients love it. She loves it. And ultimately it works well for the business. That's a win-win-win. Remember those?

So get creative. There are ways to create the margin you need. You don't have to do the nine-to-five thing every day. There are always ways to overcome challenges on a personal and business level if you'll just look for innovative solutions.

What creative solution to a big problem is right under your nose, right now?

It's there. You just need to see it. And bring it to life.

EPILOGUE

LEAVE IT ALL ON THE COURSE

*"It is not enough to do your best; you must know what you want to do and **then** do your best."*

W. EDWARD DEMING

I have four smart, hardworking children, and I'm proud of all of them. But I want to close this book with a story about my youngest daughter, Whitney.

When Whitney was in high school, she was the captain of the lacrosse team and captain of the cross-country team. She wasn't your prototypical cross-country runner. Whitney was 5'8" and weighed 150 pounds. Most of the girls who were very good at cross-country running were much shorter than her and weighed 110 pounds. They were much faster than Whitney, but she always trained hard and kept her times in the top ten on a team that usually won the state.

During her senior year, Whitney was preparing for a big meet. She said to me, "Dad, I want to break my personal best."

Her personal best for this particular run was about 23.5 minutes. To put this time in perspective, the girls that usually won these meets had running times under 18 minutes for this course. But Whitney's goal was to beat her own personal record, and run the course in under 23 minutes.

The big meet was held at Berry College in Rome, Georgia. Perhaps eight or ten high schools participated, and hundreds of people attended it. Now, in case you've never watched a massive cross-country running meet, I'll tell you that you don't get to see a heck of a lot. From a short distance, you typically see the runners start, and then you see them finish.

During Whitney's event, my wife Indy and I made our way to a spot near the finish line, so we could wait to catch sight of our daughter. The fastest runners soon came into sight, and began crossing the finishing line in packs of eight and ten.

At about the 22-minute mark, we finally saw Whitney coming down the final stretch. I'll never forget seeing her come into view. She was clearly fighting the clock, knowing that she was approaching 23 minutes. She was running her heart out.

When she crossed the finish line, she collapsed and passed out.

Panicking, my wife and I fought to get to her, but there was a massive crowd of people slowing us down. In the few moments while we were fighting our way through, we lost sight of Whitney and she disappeared. She had quickly been taken off the course, to the medical tent. When we learned this, we found the medical tent as quickly as we could; though fighting the crowd still took several minutes. When we walked into the medical tent, we spotted Whitney lying on a stretcher. She was conscious, thank God. She was packed in ice, with a moist towel on her head.

I knelt down next to her and took her hand. It didn't cross my mind at that moment, since I was so concerned for her, but she had done it. *She had beaten her personal best.* Lying there, she knew she had done it. She later revealed that she had seen the clock and heard her time before she collapsed. Whitney had crossed the finished line in just under 23 minutes.

I held her hand gingerly, just hoping she was all right.

"Whitney, are you okay?" I asked.

"Dad, if I don't pass out when I cross the finish line, I feel like I didn't leave it all on the course," she replied.

That's a great metaphor for the kind of dedication you can have when you've achieved total clarity and identified your unique genius and found true purpose and passion in your life. It's the dedication we owe our families. It's the dedication we owe our careers. It's the dedication we owe the people whom we care about the most.

We only run this course once. We need to give it *our* personal best, and that will require everything we've got. Finding clarity, purpose and passion in your life is the best way for you to give everything you were meant to give, and reap all the rewards and satisfaction you were meant to receive.

Now, go and make it happen.

And remember; *leave it all on the course.*

CLARITY doesn't end with a single book

Continue on your path towards personal excellence and lifelong fulfillment with the virtual coach program. It takes the principles you learned in this book and goes into more detail and has additional tools and exercises to keep you operating at your peak in all areas of life. Regardless of where you live or work, you can tap into the ongoing power of these time tested principles with a minimum investment and on your own time schedule.

Materials now available online.

You will gain access immediately after registering!

Learn & Plan

Learn, plan, practice and implement these life-changing concepts at your own pace when it's convenient for you. No travel. No workshops to attend. No schedule conflicts. If I can't be with you in person, this is the next best thing.

Anchored in time tested, core principles,
The Secrets of the Top 1% equips you to:

1. Clarify your most important goals.
2. Organize your life in alignment with your top values
3. Define your goals in such a way that you will naturally accelerate your progress
4. Stay on track, focused and free of distractions
5. Overcome procrastination and other potential-limiting behaviors
6. Maximize physical, mental and emotional energy
7. Reduce stress, tension and worry
8. Refine your unique strengths
9. Build Unstoppable Self-Confidence for the right risks
10. Eliminate Clutter and other junk that bogs you down
11. Upgrade your earning, investing and giving

The *Secrets of the Top 1%* Program includes the following digital downloads:

- The Portable Coach™ 90 Day Planning System
- The Weekly Coach™ 7 Day Planning System
- Secrets of The Top 1% Workbook
  134 pages of time-tested, hands-on, action-driven learning!

In addition you'll receive the following audio messages in MP3 format:

1: **Secrets of The Top 1%**
Join The Magnificent Minority

2: **Getting Results Part 1**
Design Your Environment

3: **Getting Results Part 2**
Manufacturer Positive Expectations

4: **Unleash Your Genius**
Live The Life God Gave You

5: **The Power of Goals**
Own Your Future – Today

6: **The Power of Goals – THINKshop™**
Experience Goals Gone Wild

7: **The Mental Edge**
Win at The Mental Game of Life

8: **The Right People**
Turbo Charge Your Results With Strategic Relationships

9: **More With Less**
Lose The Baggage and Set Yourself Free

10: **Maximum Energy**
Plug Your Top 10 Energy Leaks

11: **The Portable Coach™**
Finally...The Track to Run On

PLUS:
These One-of-A-Kind Extras

- Bonus MP3: The Weekly Coach™ Accountability
  Warning: Your Comfort Zone Ends Here!
- Bonus MP3: Advanced Mental Programming
  Train Your Mind Like A Champion

With this advanced training system, Steve Cesari helps you build instant momentum and equips you to take command of yourself and your future. As a special thanks to readers of this book, when you go to **www.vitalvisionsinc.com** and enter the promo code, CLARITY, *you will save $100 on registration.*

ABOUT THE AUTHOR

Steve Cesari is the President of Vital Visions (www.vitalvisions.com), a company dedicated to equip, empower and bring clarity to individuals and organizations, in order to maximize the desired results. He has over 30 years of business experience and has launched or owned 17 companies in 8 different industries. In 1989, Steve started Trillium Heath Products, marketers of the Juiceman Juicer. In 1992, Trillium was ranked by *Inc.* magazine as one of the fastest growing, privately held companies in the US and in that same year, Steve was nominated by Inc. magazine as "Entrepreneur of the Year." He has been featured on TV and radio and has been the subject of articles in *The Wall Street Journal, Fortune, USA Today* and *Success*. Steve resides with his wife Indy in WaterSound, Florida and Atlanta, Georgia. They have four grown children.

BOOK STEVE CESARI TO BRING CLARITY TO YOUR EVENT

With Steve Cesari as your next speaker, your group will be engaged, encouraged and equipped to take on business and life with a new CAN DO attitude! Blending his personal and professional experiences, Steve's presentations are content-rich, thought provoking and full of usable, result-producing ideas. He is a dynamic speaker with a refreshing and unforgettable message delivered in a style that makes it easy to connect.

Steve Cesari is a leading expert on health, high-performance, and entrepreneurial effectiveness. As President of Vital Visions Inc, Steve's passion is to **Equip, Empower** and bring **Clarity** to individuals and organizations through his books, program's, speaking and consulting.

Visit **www.VitalVisionsInc.com** for more information.

"I have heard many speakers in my 30 years of Fortune 500 business experience, but none as compelling as Steve. He has the unique ability to share life and business experiences that result in true reflection and change in both your business and personal life."

BRUCE HANFT, REALTOR, JENNY PRUITT & ASSOCIATES

"Steve is authentic, real, and connects easily with the audience. He is genuine, thus believable...his lessons learned have broad applications for business and personal relationships."

SUSAN CARLSON, INTERNATIONAL ORGANIZATION OF CEOS

How can you use this book?

MOTIVATE

EDUCATE

THANK

INSPIRE

PROMOTE

CONNECT

Why have a custom version of *Clarity?*

- Build personal bonds with customers, prospects, employees, donors, and key constituencies
- Develop a long-lasting reminder of your event, milestone, or celebration
- Provide a keepsake that inspires change in behavior and change in lives
- Deliver the ultimate "thank you" gift that remains on coffee tables and bookshelves
- Generate the "wow" factor

Books are thoughtful gifts that provide a genuine sentiment that other promotional items cannot express. They promote employee discussions and interaction, reinforce an event's meaning or location, and they make a lasting impression. Use your book to say "Thank You" and show people that you care.

CPSIA information can be obtained at www.ICGtesting.com
Printed in the USA
239642LV00004B/1/P

9 781599 322148